Views Beyond Perception

VIEWS BEYOND PERCEPTION

Based on Buddhist Teachings

Bhante Ethkandawaka Saddhajeewa

Foreword by Bhante Dr. Henepola Gunaratana

Published by Linus Learning.
Ronkonkoma, NY 11779

ISBN 10: 1-60797-666-8
ISBN 13: 978-1-60797-666-0

Library of Congress Cataloging -in -Publication Data

Saddhajeewa,Ethkandawaka, 1974- author.
Views Beyond Perception: Based on Buddhist Teachings/Bhante Saddhajeewa.

Includes bibliographical reference and index.

I. Buddhism-Way of Life. 2. Views. I. Title.

Printed in Sri Lanka.
This book is printed on woodfree paper.

Cover design by Dharsana Senaratna- Photography by Ron Hamilton
Editorial support by Sheila Sussman

All proceeds from royalties are in support of ESA Foundation in Sri Lanka, which offers help on a sliding scale to students from kindergarten to university level who is struggling from lack of adequate facilities.

Print Number 5 4 3 2 1

CONTENTS

Acknowledgments vii

Foreword ix

01. A Universal Teaching 1

02. Buddhism and Religion 5

03. Ending Suffering 9

04. The Goal of Buddhist Life 17

05. Cultivating Happiness 21

06. Kamma and How it Affects Us 27

07. Distinguishing Good from Bad 31

08. Merit (puñña) and Morally Good Action (kusala) 35

09. Taking Life 39

10. A Buddhist View of Assisted Suicide 43

11. Death: the Buddhist View 49

12. Mind, Thoughts, and Consciousness 57

13. Managing Stress and Anxiety 61

14. Recovery from Substance Abuse 69

15. The Path to Peace Through Buddhism 77

16. Good Health is Most Important 81

17. The Purpose and Benefits of Chanting 87

18. Mindfulness at Table 91

19. Earning a Living 95

20. Marriage and Divorce 99

21. Gender Difference in Buddhism 107

Index 111

ACKNOWLEDGMENTS

In this book you will find different ideas and thoughts about life. Knowledge is conventional, but truth is truth and there is no second. Living as a Bhikku and learning the Buddha's teaching, my perceptions have progressed and matured. Based on these experiences, I have written *Views Beyond Perception* to help readers find solutions for some of their life issues, and establish peace within them. Growing up, we had many opportunities to receive advice about life, but as adults, we have to use wisdom for a better life.

In finishing *Views Beyond Perception,* there were many who gave me invaluable assistance, and I would like to share my happiness with them all. First, I would like to thank our great teacher Bhante Henepola Gunaratana; his advice and teaching has been very important. This book would never have come to fruition without the assistance of Sheila Sussman, one of my English teachers since my arrival on Long Island. My very good friend, Mr. Athula Seneviratna, has helped me considerably with corrections, suggestions, and encouragement along the way. I would also like to thank Bhante Nanda for his support and encouragement. I am grateful to Mr. Sunil Herath and Linus Publications for accepting to publish this work, and once again to Mr. Roshan Mandalawatta and Lakmalee Printers, who have printed all my previous publications.

Finally, I would like to thank Stony Brook University Social Welfare faculty professors and my friend Laura Chiusano, who helped me develop my therapeutic knowledge and social work experiences. Without mentioning the names of all my friends and others who have helped me to finish this, I would like to extend my good wishes to them all and invite them to share my happiness. May all beings be well, happy and peaceful.

Thank you,

Bhante Ethkandawaka Saddhajeewa

Long Island Buddhist Meditation Center
5, Baylis Ave
Port Jefferson
NY 11777
07.02.2016
saddhajeewa@yahoo.com

FOREWORD

Despite thriving modern scientific and technological advancement, Buddhism is gaining ground in every nook and corner of the world. Buddhist philosophy, Buddhist morals and ethics, and above all, Buddhist meditation, particularly Vipassana meditation, are gaining more and more popularity. Modern scientists, psychologists, psychotherapists and psychoanalysts are doing more and more research to find and understand the secret of the success of Buddhist practice. As it spreads all over the world without the help of large financial backing, political power, charismatic leaders, or a powerful propaganda machine, more and more people are becoming ever more curious about the secret of the supremely enlightened Buddha's peaceful teachings in this restless, sensuality-oriented world.

As the message is clear and its benefits are immediately effective and powerful, people naturally follow it willingly. Buddha's message delivers what the times call for. This is a crucial time in human history when the Dhamma is absolutely necessary to balance the lives of people living in these very chaotic modern times, and to bring them solace and comfort.

On the one hand, there are a great deal of complaints about the degenerating ethics and moral leadership in the field of religion and in secular society, and on the other hand, there is a great and absolute need for well-disciplined Buddhist leaders to take up this challenge.

The Buddha's message is loud and clear. So long as counterfeit gold does not appear in the market, pure and genuine gold will not disappear. When counterfeit gold appears in the market, pure gold disappears. Similarly, as Buddhism continues its rapid spread, the chance of mushrooming pseudo Buddhism and fake Buddhist meditation can gain ground.

One day the Venerable Mahākassapa asked the Buddha, "Venerable sir, what is the reason, what is the cause, why formerly there were fewer training rules but more Bhikkhus were established in final knowledge, while now there are more training rules but fewer Bhikkhus are established in final knowledge?"

"That's the way it is, Kassapa. When beings are deteriorating and the true Dhamma is disappearing, there are more training rules but fewer Bhikkhus are established in final knowledge. Kassapa, the true Dhamma does not disappear so long as a counterfeit of the true Dhamma has not arisen in the world. But when a counterfeit of the true Dhamma arises in the world, then the true Dhamma disappears.

"Just as, Kassapa, gold does not disappear so long as counterfeit gold has not arisen in the world, but when counterfeit gold arises then true gold disappears, so the true Dhamma does not disappear so long as a counterfeit of the true Dhamma has not arisen in the world, but when a counterfeit of the true Dhamma arises in the world, then the true Dhamma disappears. "It is not the earth element, Kassapa, that causes the true Dhamma to disappear, nor the water element, nor the heat element, nor the air element. It is the senseless people who arise right here who cause the true Dhamma to disappear.[1]

---

1 *SN. II (Nidāna Saṅyutta, Nidānavagga, 225; Connected Discourses of the Buddha, A Translation of the Saṅyuttaa Nikāya, The Book of Causation, By Bhikkhu Bodhi, 680*

"The true Dhamma does not disappear all at once in the way a ship sinks." Then the Buddha gave five reasons for the disappearance of true Dhamma. If monks, nuns, laymen and laywomen live without reverence towards the (i) Buddha, (ii) Dhamma, (iii) Saṅgha, (iv) moral training, and (v) concentration, then true Dhamma disappears. So in order to protect Dhamma, monks, nuns, laymen and laywomen should respect the Buddha, Dhamma, Saṅgha, ethical training and concentration.

People ask whether Buddhism is a philosophy, science, psychology, ethical teaching, or a way of life, but we don't have to debate on any of this. You find answers to these questions when you see the qualities of the Dhamma, which are listed in the most popular passage: "Well expounded is the Dhamma by the Sublime One, directly visible, unaffected by time, calling one to come and see, leading onwards, to be realized by the wise."

Dhamma is well expounded in the sense that its beginning is excellent, the middle is excellent and the end is excellent. The beginning is morality (*sīla*), the middle is concentration (*samādhi*) and the end is wisdom (*paññā*)—the three pillars of the Buddha's teaching. When you observe moral and ethical principles, you can gain concentration easily. With good concentration you can see things as they truly are. When you see things as they really are, wisdom arises in you naturally.

All this is directly discernable without anybody's support or interference. This is your own personal experience. What you directly experience does not need any interpretation.

As the truth exists eternally, whether the Buddhas come into existence or not, it is not affected by time. What were true billions of eons ago is true today. It will be true through eternity. It will never change. That is the nature of the truth.

Truth invites you to "Come and see." Whether you call it philosophy or psychology or science or a way of life or the Middle Path, you are the only one who can see and know what it is. Let me put it in a very pragmatic sense. Suppose you receive an invitation to "Come and see." You would ask, "Who is inviting me?" "Where should I go?" "What will I see?"

1. ***Three questions:***

   i. "Who invites us?"

   ii. "Where should we go?"

   iii. "And what will we see?"

2. ***Three answers:***

   i. "Nobody."

   ii. "Nowhere."

   iii. "See Dhamma."

3. ***What is Dhamma?***

   Anicca, dukkha, and anatta. These are the eternal elements of Dhamma.[2] They translate respectively as impermanence or change, suffering or unsatisfactoriness, and not self or insubstantiality.

We must come and see what we have within us with mindfulness and clear comprehension, and should not let go of whatever it is without investigating it. Do we have greed, hatred, delusion, imaginations, fantasies, daydreams,

---

2 *Dhammadhātu*

planning for the future, dwelling on the past, and other such preoccupations in us?

When we receive this invitation to "Come and see" we should ask "Who invites us?" "Where should we go?" "And what will we see?"

When we ask "Who invites us?" the reply comes to us, "nobody." When we ask the next question, "Where should we go?" the reply comes to us, "nowhere." Finally, when we ask the third question, "And what will we see?" we receive the answer "See the Dhamma." How and where can we see the eternal Dhamma? We do not see it as something out there in the world. So, if the invitation does not come from somebody, if we do not go somewhere to see something out in the world, then what does "Come and see" mean?

This invitation comes from Dhamma itself. It is Dhamma that asks us to "Come and see." The Dhamma that is in us invites us to "Come" close to our own heart and mind. "See" means investigate. Investigate what? Investigate Dhamma. Where is the Dhamma to investigate? Dhamma is within us. We are Dhamma. The statement "All dhammas are without self[3]," means, according to the Dhammapada commentary, that all the five aggregates are Dhamma. Our body, feeling, perceptions, thoughts, and consciousness are all.

Dhamma invites us:

It simply means that the truth in you, or what you experience all the time, constantly invites your attention to it. The truth that we experience all the time is called Dhamma—wholesome, unwholesome, neutral or imperturbable. It is this Dhamma that we experience all the time, that invites

---

3 *sabbe dhammā anattā*

us saying, "Look at me, look at me, don't ignore me. If you ignore me, you will be in trouble. If you want to be free from trouble, look at me. Take care of me."

Dhamma within us talks to us all the time. We have ears but we don't hear this message. We are deaf. We have eyes but we don't see the Dhamma. We are blind. We go on ignoring it. This is ignorance. We don't know that it is there. Our attention is somewhere else. Wherever we go there it is. Dhamma is there. It goes with us. In spite of the fact that we ignore it, Dhamma goes with us. We cannot separate ourselves from Dhamma.

The Buddha said that there are beings that have little dust in their eyes. When the Buddha started teaching the Dhamma, those who had little dust in their eyes began to feel an itch in their eyes. Then they wiped out that dust. They scratched that itch. It went away and they saw Dhamma. They saw light shining on Dhamma. That is what happened to Siddhartha Gotama himself. When the dust in his eyes was wiped out, he saw the light. He said in the first sermon, "Light arose in me. Wisdom arose in me. Knowledge arose in me." With that light he saw Dhamma in ten thousand world systems.

To represent these ten thousand world systems, Chinese Buddhists in San Francisco have named their temple ''City of Ten Thousand Buddhas'' and have installed ten thousand Buddha images.

Whether the Buddhas come to this world or not, this established Dhamma, this element of Dhamma, this law of Dhamma exists. The Buddhas realized it and comprehended it. Having realized it and having comprehended it, they taught it, pointed it out, established it, opened it, analyzed it, and made it known to the world. What is this Dhamma? All conditioned things are impermanent, all conditioned things are unsatisfactory and all dhammas are without self. There is the Dhamma that exists whether the Buddhas come into existence or not. That Dhamma is Dependent Origination. In summarizing Dependent Origination, the Buddha says,

"This, this being - this comes to be

With the arising of this - this arises

This not being - this does not come to be

With the cessation of this – this ceases.[4]"

He accepted the invitation of Dhamma. He followed the path of Dhamma. He saw the end of the repetition of birth and death. Here "See" is metaphorical. Dhamma is not something we can see with our eyes. Dhamma is an experience. Although we experience Dhamma all the time, due to our ignorance we do not know Dhamma. Not knowing Dhamma, we become even more ignorant. We are ignorant because either we do not pay mindful attention to Dhamma, or we pay unmindful attention to it, blind attention to it, or superficial attention to it. When we are blinded with emotion, greed, hate, fear, and confusion, we cannot pay attention to the reality underneath the emotion, greed, hate, fear, and confusion. We are blinded with emotion; we are biased and judgmental or critical. We can see the injustice and unfairness of others, but we don't see our own bias and injustice. We even may say that we practice Dhamma and the other person is pretending to practice Dhamma, that he or she is not honest.

---

4 *"Iti imasmiṃ sati idaṃ hoti,*
imassuppādā idaṃ uppajjati
imasmiṃ asati idaṃ na hoti,
imassa nirodhā idaṃ nirujjhati." (MN. III, Bahudhātuka sutta)

How and where can we see Dhamma? If it does not come from somebody, if we do not go somewhere to find it and if we do not see something out in the world, then what does "Come and see" mean?

***Sabbe dhammā anattā* --** All dhammas (conditioned or unconditioned things) are not self.

Here 'all' means all the five aggregates. That is all we have. All of them are in a state of flux. They must be renewed all the time in order to keep them alive. Why should they renew themselves all the time? Because they—body, feelings, perceptions, thoughts, and consciousness—wear out. This wearing out is called impermanence. As they wear out, they must be renewed so that they can survive. This is the nature of all conditioned things (*saṅkhāra*). They must be repeated, repaired, renewed, and amended. This change or this impermanence is taking place within us all the time. We should "come and see" this change as it is. The Buddha asked us to get intimately close to this nature and see this nature with wisdom. This is "come and see."

When the mind is influenced by anger, hate, jealousy, confusion and greed friendship changes into animosity and rivalry. Friends fight with friends. Children fight with parents. Parents fight with children. Siblings fight with siblings. Relatives fight with relatives. Teachers fight with students. Students fight with teachers. Neighbors fight with neighbors. Nations fight with nations. Countries fight with countries. Meditators fight with meditators. Dhamma teachers fight with Dhamma teachers. Men fight with women. Women fight with men. Boys fight with girls. Girls fight with boys. Boys fight with boys. Girls fight with girls. Nobody escapes fighting with one another so long as their minds are obsessed by anger, hate, jealousy, confusion and greed. One who "Comes and sees" Dhamma certainly can see this situation within himself or herself. If we learn and teach Dhamma as an academic subject, we will never "Come and see" Dhamma.

When the mind is free from greed, hatred and delusion, even for a fraction of a second, we experience peace. We must "Come and see" this experience of peace at the moment greed is abandoned. We must "Come and see" our experience of peace at the moment hatred is abandoned. We must "Come and see" when we have mental impurities, when we experience pain, and we must "Come and see" when we abandon them and we experience peace and happiness. This is "Come and see." So, Dhamma within us invites us to "Come and see." We don't need anybody to ask us to see what is happening within ourselves. We must get inside us, look inside us, experience this nature within us, understand it and have clear comprehension of this phenomenon. This is "Come and see." We must build up this habit to "Come and see" what really happening in us without trying to point our finger at others. Pointing our finger at others is against the principle of "Come and see".

The Buddha realized it and taught it to the world and passed away. This is the eternal truth that we experience at any moment in our life. Nobody, no god, no human, no Mara can make impermanence permanence; suffering non-suffering; non-self, self. Impermanence remains impermanence, suffering remains suffering, and non-self remains non-self. Seeing this nature with wisdom we liberate ourselves from suffering. That we can "Come and see."

> "Here, Upavāna, having seen a form with the eye, a bhikkhu experiences the form as well as lust for the form. He understands that lust for forms exists internally, thus:

'There is in me lust for forms internally.' Since that is so, Upavāna, the Dhamma is directly visible, immediate, inviting one to come and see, applicable to be personally experienced by the wise.

Further, Upavāna, having heard a sound with the ear… having cognized a mental phenomenon with the mind, a bhikkhu experiences the mental phenomenon as well as lust for the mental phenomenon. He understands that lust for mental phenomenon exists internally thus: 'There is in me lust for mental phenomena internally.' Since that is so, Upavāna, the Dhamma is directly visible, immediate, inviting one to come and see, applicable to be personally experienced by the wise.

But here, Upavāna, having seen a form with the eye, a bhikkhu experiences the form without experiencing lust for the form. He understands that lust for forms does not exist internally thus: 'There is in me no lust for forms internally.' Since that is so, Upavāna, the Dhamma is directly visible, immediate, inviting one to come and see, applicable to be personally experienced by the wise.

Further, Upavāna, having heard a sound with the ear… having cognized a mental phenomenon with the mind, a bhikkhu experiences the mental phenomenon without experiencing lust for the mental phenomenon. He understands that lust for mental phenomena does not exist internally thus: 'there is in me no lust for mental phenomena internally. Since that is so, Upavāna, the Dhamma is directly visible, immediate, inviting one to come and see, applicable to be personally experienced by the wise."[5]

---

5 *S. IV, 41-42;CDB. By BB. 1155*

Everything that we know is Dhamma

Our bodies are in a state of flux. They must be renewed all the time in order to keep us alive. Why should they renew themselves all the time? Because they—body, feelings, perceptions, thoughts, and consciousness—wear out. This wearing out is called impermanence. As they wear out, they must be renewed so that they can survive. This is the nature of all conditioned things. They must be repeated, repaired, and amended. This change or this impermanence is taking place within us all the time. We should "come and see" this change as it is. The Buddha asked us to get intimately close to this nature and see this nature with wisdom. This is "come and see."

This constant change of everything is very painful.

This constant change of everything is very painful. There is no way to stop this change. This happens from the moment we were conceived in our mothers' wombs. We have different names for this change. Sometimes we call it growth, old age, decay, or death. We die every moment and it is called momentary death. We are made up of more than a hundred trillion cells. Every cell in our body dies and a new cell is born every moment. Every feeling dies and a new feeling arises. Every perception dies and a new perception arises. Every thought dies and a new thought arises. Every moment of consciousness dies and a new moment of consciousness arise. Whether the Buddha comes into the world or not this established Dhamma exists. This is what we should "come and see."

We should "come and see" that in this repetition of birth and death of body, feelings, perception, thoughts, and consciousness nothing remains unchanged. There is nothing permanent in these aggregates of clinging. This is what "come and see." We come very close to this very nature and become one with it to see it as it is. Becoming intimate with these three aspects—impermanence, suffering, and selflessness—of established Dhamma is what is called "Come and See."

See how senses and their objects interact:

Also, when senses and sensory objects come in contact there arises series of thought moments. Some of them turn out to be lustful thoughts, some hateful thoughts, jealous thoughts, thoughts full of fear, or thoughts of cruelty. We know these thoughts at that very moment they arise. We can feel them at that very moment. Meeting senses and sensory objects is Dhamma. Feeling arising from this contact is Dhamma. Thoughts arising through this contact are Dhamma. Reaction to the thoughts is Dhamma. We can see them happening right within ourselves. We should be fully engaged in knowing them. We should be intimately involved in knowing them. We should be fully aware of their occurrence in us. This is "Come and see."

When greed arises we experience pain.

When greed arises we experience pain. When greed fades away we feel relief of pain. We should come and see this very nature of greed and absence of greed. When hatred arises we feel pain. When hatred fades away we experience joy. We should "come and see" this very nature of hatred and joy. When fear, tension, worry, and anxiety arise we are in pain. When they disappear we are relieved of that pain. We should "come and see" this very nature of these mental states.

When the mind is free from negatives:

I must "Come and see" the truth of suffering, the truth of the cause of suffering, the truth of the end of suffering, and the truth of the steps to ending suffering—all within myself. These are called the Four Noble Truths. I must see this logical unit within me. This is what I experience all the time. So long as I focus my mind on others' greed, hate, ego, jealousy, fear, anxiety and tension, I do not see the cause of my suffering within me. Suffering does not have an owner. It simply exists within me. I must look at it honestly. Then I must try to understand how by cultivating Right Thinking I can get rid of my suffering. I must straighten my thought. If I think with lots of greed, I suffer. Then I think of letting go of my greed. That is my thought of generosity. It reduces my suffering. If I cultivate a hateful thought, I suffer. Then I think of letting go of my hate. This is my thought of loving-friendliness. It reduces my suffering. If I think a cruel thought, I suffer. Then I think of letting go of my cruel thought. That is my compassion. It reduces my suffering. So I must think of letting go of my greed, hatred, and cruelty so that I can experience the relief of tension caused by greed, hatred and cruelty.

Letting go of my greed, hatred and cruelty

Occasional thinking of letting go of my greed, hatred and cruelty is not enough. I must think of letting go of them every day, every hour, and every minute. If I keep thinking of preventing them from arising, then I can prevent them from arising. If they arise, in spite of my earnest wish to hold them at bay, they can come back. Then I must think of overcoming them, weakening them, chastising them, and getting rid of them. As they weaken or fade away, I must get help from my skillful thinking.

Letting go of my thought of greed is my generosity. When I cultivate and nourish the thought of generosity and think skillfully, I strangle and suffocate greed. I let go of the thought of hatred and I cultivate and nourish the thought of loving friendliness. When I cultivate and nourish the thought of loving friendliness and think skillfully, I strangle and suffocate the thought of hatred. I cultivate and nourish the thought compassion and I let go of the thought of cruelty. When I cultivate and nourish the thought of compassion and think skillfully, I strangle and suffocate the thought of cruelty.

Meaningful speech:

Then, with the thought of generosity, you should tell the truth, speak cordially, softly and gently, and say meaningful things. As you speak this way, you reduce your suffering and experience happiness. You do not regret saying the right thing or a beneficial thing, thing that brings harmony and peace. When you tell lies and speak maliciously, you damage somebody's name and reputation or your own name and reputation. Or you worry with embarrassment about the thing that you have said. With the thought of generosity, you show your friendliness and compassion to all living beings and are happy to see them relaxed and alive in good health. With the thought of generosity, friendliness, and compassion you abstain from stealing and sexual misconduct. With the thought of generosity, friendliness, and compassion you choose an appropriate job, so that you can work together with others in friendliness and compassion.

Support your mindfulness training:

This practice supports your mindfulness training. Then you can become even more mindful of your speech, action, thinking, and livelihood. With good mindfulness you can let go of your greed, hate, and cruelty and develop stronger thoughts of generosity, friendliness, and compassion. With this practice of mindfulness, you can gain better concentration and see your suffering even more clearly.

Make a mindful effort to understand:

This practice brings you understanding. Effort and mindfulness become strong. As they become strong, your thinking, speech, action, livelihood, effort, mindfulness, and concentration become stronger. With strong concentration you can see your suffering even more clearly than ever before. Thus you go on repeating the practice of these eight steps. Each and every time you repeat them your thoughts, speech, action, livelihood, effort, mindfulness, and concentration get purer and purer until finally you are able to overcome your ego or notion of an enduring self. All this you can see within yourself. It does not matter whether the Buddha's teaching is labeled philosophy, psychology, science, or way of life when we follow the steps he has given—Right Understanding, Right thoughts, Right speech, Right action, Right livelihood, Right effort, Right mindfulness, and Right concentration—we end up in peace and happiness. This is the message of the Buddha.

Ven. Ethkandawaka Saddhajeewa, psychotherapist and meditation teacher presents in his book his personal experience with people. He writes and comments on numerous practical aspects of Buddhism. Combining his monastic training with knowledge of western education, he is highly qualified to present the teaching of the Buddha in a most delightful style. Adapting his teaching experience to writing this book, he makes every topic in it uniquely refreshing.

Bhante Dr. Henepola Gunaratana

(Agga maha Pandith, Chief Monk of North America; Author of *Mindfulness in Plain English*)

1

A UNIVERSAL TEACHING

People are often curious when they see me going about in my monastic robes. "Are you a Buddhist monk?" they ask. "Yes, I am." And often the next question is, "Is Buddhism a religion?" The most appropriate answer I can give is, "It depends on the way you see it. By definition, a religion is a belief in, worship of, or obedience to a supernatural power or powers, or belief in a transcendent controlling power or powers. Buddhism does not fit this particular framework

Buddhism does not depend on beliefs, a creative superpower God, a gospel, or rituals. The Buddha is neither an agent of God nor the son of God; nor is he a messenger or a prophet. The Buddha spent countless years coming to understand the truth of the world, and that is what he taught his followers. The truth the Buddha realized is the truth that everyone can experience for himself or she if they apply the method he taught. Chiefly, the Buddha advised us to develop our mind, because mind is the leader and originator of all our actions. To develop a clear and enlightened mind, we are given a path to follow that covers three types of action: the first, *paññā*, is wisdom, that is, having a true understanding of reality and not deluding oneself. The second, *sīla*, is the quality of upholding morality and ethical discipline. The third is *samādhi*, concentration, the practice of quieting and focusing the mind on a single sensation or object.

When we make a positive commitment to uphold the quality of our morality and also practicing concentration, we will be able to experience wisdom. We should bear in mind that this is a process of gradual of training and therefore needs to be practiced with positive commitment, consistency, determination and courage. There are three positive activities that will help us to gradually progress on this path: generosity, morality and contemplation; put more explicitly, they are practicing generosity, observing moral precepts, and progressing in meditation. By practicing generosity, we can reduce our greed and unwholesome desires. We can practice generosity three ways: by giving knowledge, giving consumables, and giving life. Even a simple action like giving someone directions is giving knowledge, when the directions are given with compassion. As human beings, we all have to follow some rules of conduct and guidance, those commonly accepted by the society in which we live. Beyond that, in general, if we can apply the five precepts for good moral conduct (not killing, not stealing, not engaging in sexual misconduct, not lying, and not using drugs and alcohol) we will develop our humanity. These precepts are applicable in any society. Meditation is the method for cultivating the mind. By cultivating the mind, we are able to see things as they actually are. This way, we develop a broad mind instead of a narrow mind. The mind has an enormous perceptive capacity, and we will discover this more and more the longer we practice meditation. We will be able to control our senses relating to anger, hatred, lust, delusion and greed and this leads to experiencing less stress, anxiety, and depression.

There was once a monk who used to wander the streets as his daily routine. A rich young man noticed this monk walking about every day. He noticed that the monk never had an angry expression and was never in a hurry. The monk was calm and serene. It puzzled that rich young man because he was experiencing a stressful life, but the monk apparently enjoyed a calm and peaceful life. So the rich young man decided to talk to that monk. One day he approached the monk and asked a question: what was the secret of that peaceful and calm lifestyle? He begged for some advice so that he might enjoy the same peace and calm in his own life. The monk knew the young man was not a Buddhist; therefore the advice he gave was ordinary, applicable in day-to-day life. The first piece of advice was, "Dear friend, when you get up in the early morning, think of helping somebody who comes to you asking for assistance. It might be a beggar, it might be a visitor, or it might be one of your servants; whoever it is doesn't matter. The main thing is to think of something to give them." The rich young man started to follow this method the very next day. He began to feel less harried than previously. A few weeks later, he again approached the monk and described his experiences. "Reverend Sir, I applied your method. Now I feel happy. I would like to ask you for more advice. Please make another suggestion." The next advice the monk gave him was to constantly think about the good qualities of superior human beings. The young man began to consider the nine conventional qualities of a superior human being: accomplished worth, perfect self-enlightenment, knowledge of proper conduct, beneficial speech, blissful knowledge of the worlds, perfect character fulfillment, offering of guidance to people, transformative wisdom, and charisma. A few weeks later, he approached the monk again and described his experiences. The young man told the monk that he was now very happy and very peaceful. Situations that previously caused him to become angry could no longer make him angry. "I have peace, my family has peace, and the places around me have peace. Also, people around me have happy thoughts about me, and they appreciate me. I would like to continue. Please advise me further." The monk's next advice to the young rich man was to observe morality. The young man started to observe the basic five precepts already mentioned. Now he was putting three things into practice: generosity, discipline, and meditation. A few weeks later, he again reported his experiences, his happiness and his peace to the monk, and expressed his gratitude. From this story, we can see that stress and anxiety arise from greed, anger, and delusion, and that the antidotes are generosity, discipline and meditation. If we can reduce our greed and other defilements, we will be able to develop peace and happiness the same way this young person did.

I also practice these three actions, generosity, discipline and meditation, to reduce my stress and anxiety, and also to develop my wisdom. My goal is to achieve wisdom. To this end, I need to cultivate a happy and peaceful life. Therefore, I practice generosity, I observe precepts, and I practice meditation. I don't pray to any gods or to any superpower to do this for me. I am not developing a set of beliefs. I am not dependent on beliefs. By practicing generosity, observing precepts and meditation, I examine, I investigate, I study. As a result, my life is peaceful and less stressful. I am developing some worthy qualities as a result of these practices, and am able to be straight, upright, obedient, gentle and humble. Other qualities I am developing at the same time are contentment, a simple life with few duties, a life without stress, with self-control, discretion, and respect and equal treatment of all beings. It is useless to pray to a superpower for these qualities. The best method is to apply the method the Buddha taught, which I do. So according to this clarification, I do not have a religion. I follow all good teachings without giving them a specific label.

2

BUDDHISM AND RELIGION

When religion is the subject of discussion, it is hard to avoid talking about God, and by this we usually mean a Creator God. Most cultures explain the world's existence through creation stories, and they venerate a god or gods who can intervene on behalf of living beings. God is the focus of several of the world's major religions whose adherents accept this view on faith. When we see or hear about volcanoes, earthquakes, tsunamis, floods, wildfires, and other natural disasters occurring around the world, shall we say that God is behind these, too? If God brings such misery and hardship to living beings, what kind of faith should we have in such a God?

The Buddha, on the other hand, described the nature of the world as a beginning less and endless process of expansion and contraction[6]. The Buddhist view is that the world undergoes expansion and contraction as a consequence of a natural process, and at times the outcome may be destructive. We are unable to prevent these occurrences. In fact, due to thoughtless human activity, we humans can cause even more destruction and disasters.

6 *Agganna sutta*

The Buddha's teaching focuses on giving us a direct path to end the suffering we experience in life, or at the very least, alleviate it. On that path, seeking answers to classic questions like, "Was the universe created?" is irrelevant. Though perhaps interesting to know, such knowledge does nothing to alleviate suffering[7]. The downside is that while keeping our minds occupied with such questions, we so clutter our minds that they have no opportunity calm down.

In the teachings of the Buddha, all things in this world, whether seen or unseen, are subject to three conditions: arising, decaying and departing. When things arise, we see that things have arisen, but the history behind their occurrence isn't immediately obvious. That is because our range of vision is not wide or deep enough to see the hidden histories.

In Buddhist teachings, all physical material is composed of four natural elements: earth, air, fire and water. What we see appears differently according to the proportion of those elements contained in the object of observation. As an example, we see a chair differently from a bottle of water. We may see the water in the water bottle, but not the water in the chair. Similarly, when we see a pool of water or a bottle of water, we are not likely to perceive the presence of the earth, fire, or air elements in them, because the water element is so much more abundant than the other three elements. Yet, if we look with insight, we will recognize that the other elements are there, although in lesser proportion to the water element. We also perceive a pool of water differently from a bottle of water. It is so because, although the water element is predominant in both, there is much more water in the pool than in the bottle of water. We need the insight to have similar regard for the air, earth, and fire elements that are also present in the pool or the bottle of water, no matter in what proportions the elements occur.

---

7 *Culamalukya Sutta*

Believing ideas or accepting conjectures without having arrived at measurable evidence to verify them is contrary to the methods of scientific inquiry and, likewise, contrary to the methods of Buddhist inquiry. If I am to believe that God created the world, further questions necessarily arise, such as, where did God come from? Who or what created God? When I look at the world from a scientific or logical perspective, I cannot grasp that the universe is the work of a Creator God. I want to study the nature of the world, its life and purpose, but I can't just put my faith in others' beliefs and conjectures. What Buddhists are encouraged to do is investigate and discover the truth for themselves. It is better to ground oneself in deep understanding acquired through personal experience and realization rather than form beliefs through hearsay.

The Buddha became a teacher after his enlightenment 2,600 years ago in India. He advised his monks to take his teachings as their guide in his place after his death. Even today we do not have a world leader of Buddhism. Our leader is the Buddha's teaching, the *Dhamma*. However, we do have Buddhist community *(sangha)* leaders. They lead only the community, not the dispensation or relaxation of the rules of the Buddha. No one can change or edit Buddha's teaching. In following the teaching, Buddhists use confidence based on knowledge, and wisdom rather than belief. They don't depend on a: superpower, divine messages or miracles. Following the teaching means they have to be 'lamps unto themselves' and apply determination, mindfulness, pure conduct, discrimination, self-restraint, right living and vigilance. As disciples, we are encouraged to investigate and debate in order to develop our wisdom. Those who apply this method find their good reputation increases, and they go from brightness to brightness.

3

ENDING SUFFERING

Nibbana is a state of mind that we can develop. It is a state of comprehension and understanding. It is not something we can gain after death. Only humans can attain *Nibbana* through comprehending the true nature of the world. It is the result of a long process of training and cultivation. In the same way that a student who wants to pursue a university degree first has to pass from playgroup to kindergarten, then through elementary school, middle school and high school before entering university and finally graduating, so *Nibbana* is not easily gained. If a person engages continuously with their academic studies, for example, they will eventually attain their desired qualification. *Nibbana* is the goal for Buddhists and requires long and difficult preparation. For that, they have to have ambition, they have to have courage, and they have to work hard. A person who has the goal of attaining *Nibbana* must lead a life in which eventually all mental defilements are removed. That becomes their duty and obligation. Finally, through developing their mind, they can experience the state of freedom and clarity of mind that is *Nibbana. Nibbana* is a Pali word. Ni means no and Vana means blowing, hence, not fanning greed and desire, but extinguishing those fires. *Nibbana* means a state of mind without desire and without anger or any other defilement, where the mind remains clear, pure and bright.

We have five faculties. We use these five faculties to perceive objects. We have eyes; we use these eyes to see images. We have ears; we use them to hear sounds. The object of the nose is smell. The object of the tongue is taste. The object of the body is touch or feeling. When these faculties and come into contact with there sense objects, they also connect with consciousness. Because of this mental connection, when we perceive objects, we perceive them as either good or bad. In other words, we accept or reject the sense objects, and form opinions about them. Similarly, when we hear sounds, we perceive them as beautiful or harsh. When tasting things, we perceive them as delicious or unpleasant. When smelling things, we perceive them as fragrant or malodorous. When touching things, we perceive them as smooth or rough, hot or cold, etc. According to Buddhist teaching, we fall into these two ways of perceiving because of our deluded mind. If we were to realize the true nature of these objects, we would not take sense contact this way. A person who has attained *Nibbana* always maintains a neutral attitude towards sense objects; he or she does not accept or reject a thing because of its nature. As worldly beings, we are in the habit of forming *Upadana*, that is, clinging or attachment. We accumulate mental formations in our mind. Whether we have beautiful or ugly mental formations, whether we accept or reject an object, we are accumulating mental defilements. A person who has attained *Nibbana* will neither accept nor reject sense objects because he or she understands the nature of the object, and will have neutral feelings about it. They will see things just as they are and hear things just as they are, without forming opinions or judgments in mind about them.

According to the Buddha's word, someone who is mindful will be someone who can follow the Middle Way.

When we follow the Middle Way by practicing morality, concentration, and wisdom, we will be able to attain *Nibbana* as a result of those actions. Moral discipline refers to the kinds of observances that purify our words and actions. The five precepts, the eight precepts and the ten precepts respectively are the basis for all Buddhist lay people to practice morality. By following this system, we can maintain pure words and actions, and as a result of that, we will be able to cultivate a very deep spiritual environment. If we don't use wholesome and peaceful words and actions, we will not have peace of mind. Morality and discipline help us maintain the foundation of our spiritual environment. Here, we mainly purify our actions and words. If we can purify words and actions, it will result in our ability to develop concentration. This will lead to developing our ability to avoid doing unwholesome things, even secretly. Practicing morality affords the opportunity to maintain concentration. With morality and concentration combined, we will have the opportunity to develop wisdom. By developing such an environment, we can practice generosity and meditation to develop our wisdom and understanding. If we practice these Middle Way activities, we will be able to purify our words, actions and mind; in other words, we will be able to eliminate the defilements we harbor in mind and attain *Nibbana*.

According to Buddhist teaching, we have 1,500 mental defilements. To begin to eliminate them, we first have to do certain things. A man named Alawaka once asked the Buddha how to attain *Nibbana*. The Buddha answered that to attain *Nibbana* he would have to observe precepts (moral discipline) every day and every moment. He would have to be wise. He would have to have peaceful thoughts, courage and determination. Then he would be able to practice the Middle Way, that is, right view, right intention, right speech, right action, right livelihood, right effort, right mindfulness and right concentration. This is known as the,"Noble Eightfold Path".

Right view means having a deep and wide understanding of the consequences of our actions and words. Someone who maintains right view is ready to lead a moral life. Right view requires more than simple knowledge of the general meaning of *kamma*. Right view is always based on the theory of cause and effect. Someone who holds right view does not depend on logic, nor side with optimists or pessimists; he remains a realist. Such a person is not disposed to destroy life, is not disposed to take what is not given, not disposed to misconduct in regard to sensual pleasure, does not use false, harsh or slanderous speech, nor cloud the mind with intoxicants. Finally, he or she thoroughly understands the Four Noble Truths: the truth of suffering, the cause of suffering, the cessation of suffering, and the path leading to the cessation of suffering. Such individuals become fully liberated and attain enlightenment, or *nibbana*.

To arrive at that point, at that state, they will have to apply a further seven factors to reduce their defilements. Right intention refers to the intention to renounce certain actions. It is the intention to refrain from causing, and from destroying life. If they can maintain this right intention, they will be able to create wholesome concepts as a result. When a person observes right speech, their words will be especially peaceful for all living beings. When they observe right action, that action will be helpful to all living beings. When they observe right livelihood, their life will not disturb any living beings. In the course of our lives, we have to make all kinds of efforts, but right effort is the particular kind of effort we need to strive for, because right effort is helpful both to ourselves and also to others. This means, as a whole, that there are four courses of action: we have to make the effort to prevent unwholesome states of mind from arising when they have not yet arisen, make the effort to abandon unwholesome states of mind that have already arisen, make the effort to arouse wholesome states that have not yet arisen, and finally, to make the effort to maintain wholesome states that have already arisen. Right mindfulness means maintaining wholesome thoughts all the time and performing wholesome actions. If we are mindful, we will be aware of everything we say and do. We will also be aware of what we bring about through our words and actions. Finally, we will apply right concentration. When we maintain right concentration we have a direct path to wisdom. With right concentration we will be able to see the defilements we hold in or mind, and receive the insight on how to eliminate them. We will then have established a purified mind. That mind, unlike an ordinary mind is unchanging. In putting these seven factors into practice, we will be able to always maintain this pure mind with pure thought and pure action. When we maintain that quality of concentration, our mind is alert and quick to eliminate doubts, skepticism, false beliefs, sensual craving, attachment to physical pleasure, and all other fetters and hindrances. This is the purity of mind that we can develop through our practice. It is a state of mind we develop ourselves, no one can give it to us.

The practice a person cultivates does not belong to anyone else, it belongs to him or her. No one can walk this path for us, it is for us alone. The Buddha and his teachings can be viewed as just such a path that we have to follow and experience. To apply the Middle Way to our life, we need: experience, knowledge, courage and determination. To develop all these qualities we may need a long life, because it is a long process. We don't know how long it will take for us personally. The time it takes will depend on the qualities we maintain or develop. Whoever fulfills all these qualities will be able to attain *Nibbana* or full liberation within this life. If we do not fulfill our duties, we have to make a more strenuous effort to perfect our qualities. Do not become discouraged or feel that you can't complete your development in this lifetime. Once you have attained the path, you can continue it even in the next life. The most important step is to attain the path, to practice, and prepare us.

A person who attains *Nibbana* becomes superhuman because he no longer has any defilement. He doesn't experience anger, desire or greed, and he is no longer deluded. He will always be filled with loving kindness, compassion, sympathetic joy and equanimity. All of us have these qualities in us, but they are not firmly established. We do have loving, kind, and compassionate thoughts, and we feel sympathetic joy and equanimity towards our nearest and dearest. However, because of our strong reliance on self-centered habit, we find it difficult to feel the same way towards all living beings. To reach that state we have to realize and understand true nature. The true nature of life is that all living beings are equally important through their natural interdependence on one another, the natural elements and the environment. However, to come to that realization we need to eliminate ego and all the other defilements in our mind. For that there is a process. That process is the Noble Eightfold Path, or morality, concentration, and wisdom. These three activities are interdependent: without morality there is no concentration, and without concentration there is no wisdom. Once we are prepared to apply this method, we will be able to eliminate our defilements and self-centered perspective. We will then be able to live with compassionate thoughts, loving friendliness, sympathetic joy and equanimity toward all living beings.

Siddhartha Gautama became the Buddha after having sustained a very lengthy process. As Buddhist accounts tell, he had already known twenty-five thousand Buddhas. From this we can gather how much we need to practice to tame our nature. Being Buddhist means we have to practice discipline, generosity, and meditation to develop our morality, concentration and wisdom. Those who develop these spiritualties can reach *Nibbana*. Other terms for *Nibbana* are enlightenment and awakening. *Nibbana* is not something beyond this world it is a state that we can experience ourselves in this very world. No one can attain it by worshiping a god or a Buddha. Only by practicing good and wholesome action and developing the mind can they do so. The Buddha is the teacher to guide us. He is not a maker, creator, or savior and he can't do it for us but he has shown us the way. The person whose mind is completely free from greed, anger, hatred, ignorance and delusion realizes *Nibbana*. When the mind is clear and no longer harbors any defilement, happy and peaceful thoughts arise. Such a person will never do any harm to himself or to others. His words will be peaceful and his actions peaceful and helpful for all living beings.

The Buddha distinguished four types of people. Three of these are able to comprehend the truth: some will realize it suddenly; some will arrive at an understanding with the help of explanation; and others arrive at truth with the help of further explication and the use of analogies. The fourth type are those who will not be able to understand it because they did not prepare their spiritual foundation sufficiently. The Buddha gave this analogy for these people: picture the lotus flower. Some lotuses bloom as soon as the sun falls on them; some need two or three days' sunshine to bloom, some buds need two or three weeks' sunshine to open; and some buds don't even appear – they die underwater. This illustrates that *Nibbana* is not something to be arrived at in an instant - it is the result of a long growth process. It illustrates how we, as human beings, have to use every opportunity to practice spirituality. *Nibbana* is the state of the superior human being; therefore, if our goal is to attain *Nibbana*, we must respect our humanity and live accordingly. This is very important. If our goal is to attain *Nibbana* and we also practice all these activities, we will be free from stress, anger, depression, anxiety, and other mental illnesses. Therefore, in the process, whether we attain our goal or not, we can still practice leading peaceful and happy lives.

4

THE GOAL OF BUDDHIST LIFE

Some people consider Buddhism a philosophy; many consider it a religion, while others think of it as a way of life. Whichever way they understand it doesn't matter. If we want to learn and get any result from the Buddha's teaching, we need to study it and then apply it in daily living. This way we can investigate what it means and look into it to further our understanding. The best way to describe the Buddha's teaching is as ultimate truth. Truth is truth it is universal. Buddhism doesn't belong to a particular group of people, a country or region; it is for all human beings who can think and reason. Another way to put it is to say that only the wise can benefit from Buddhism. Whether the Buddha is alive or not, Buddhism exists because it teaches the truth about the nature of the world. The Buddha's task was to revive the truth that had been covered over. The Buddha was an investigator, a researcher and a teacher.

The Buddha's goal was to understand the true nature of the world, in particular, the suffering it contains. Therefore, if someone wants to follow the Buddha's teaching and guidance, their goal should be to discover the true nature of the world and the reasons behind our suffering. According to the Buddha's teaching, the nature of the world is cyclical. There is no starting point or end point. There are three characteristics present in our world: impermanence, suffering, and interdependent existence. If we can discontinue the cycle of suffering, we will have reached the goal. To put it another way, if we can live with a good understanding of the real nature of the world, we can eliminate our mental afflictions. Doing this will allow us to cultivate a superior quality of life. The Buddha's guidance will help us, but we have to realize this nature ourselves. The Buddha is a teacher he is not a savior. He offered opportunity and methods to learn and practice, but it is then up to us whether we accept that opportunity.

As Buddhists born into this world, we have to do three things to fulfill our goal: we must do no harm, do only good, and purify our mind. According to this teaching, we must first understand what not to do. Therefore, if there is something harmful to ourselves, harmful to others, or harmful to both, that is an action we must refrain from (Ambalattika Rahulowada sutta M.N). The way to avoid doing harm is to uphold the precepts, that is, observe moral conduct. The precepts will help us to develop morality and will provide a virtuous environment for our life. Being in that virtuous environment, we can practice generosity to reduce desire, anger and ignorance. Next, if there is something useful to ourselves, useful to others, or useful to both, that is an action we should do. Finally, to control our senses, we have to develop our mind. This means reducing mental afflictions and developing a wholesome mind. The only method to do so is a strong meditation practice. Practicing meditation will help cultivate our mind. More on meditation in chapter eleven. These three activities connect directly with morality, concentration, and wisdom.

Our fundamental Buddhist ethical practice is to avoid killing, stealing, adultery, lying, and using drugs and alcohol. Through these observances we can cultivate a friendly and peaceful lifestyle. By maintaining concentration we can live mindfully. Through mindfulness, we are aware of who we are and what we are doing. By maintaining wisdom we can think deeply and widely. We can see in the present moment what results our actions will bring about. We know this life now, and also the future. We can understand *kamma* (mindful action) and the effect of *kamma*. If we cultivate this kind of character or behavior, we are living as Buddhists, whatever religion or ethnicity we belong to nominally. This means anyone can be Buddhist if they apply this method to their life. Being born into a Buddhist family does not make you a Buddhist. If you go to temple, stay with monks, and worship the Buddha, that does not make you Buddhist, but if you live mindfully, avoiding harmful activities, you are already living Buddhist life.

5

CULTIVATING HAPPINESS

Buddha's disciples are categorized into four groups: *bhikku* (monks), bhikkuni (nuns), *upasaka* (male laypersons) *upasika* (female laypersons). *Bhikku* and *bhikkuni* are those who are ordained and live in a monastery with the support of lay people. *Upasaka* and *upasika* are Buddhists living as lay people. They can have a family, and they can enjoy sensual pleasures. This means lay people can enjoy sights, sounds, tastes, touch and smell, but excessive indulgence in sensual pleasure is sure to bring trouble. According to the Buddha's *Dhammachakkapavattana Sutta*, we are advised to avoid the two extremes of self-indulgence and self-mortification. The Buddha described these extremes as being base and uncultivated, and commented that people who don't develop their mind operate from those extremes. According to Buddha's teaching, all lay people are advised to observe the five fundamental precepts. Observing the five precepts, they can have family, wealth, and enjoyments - it is not against Buddha's word.

If lay people want to cultivate their happiness, they need to uphold the Dhamma. The Buddha mentioned four kinds of accomplishments in the *Viyagghapajja Sutta* :

> Four conditions, Vyagghapajja, conduce to a householder's wealth and happiness in this very life. Which four? The accomplishment of persistent effort, the accomplishment of watchfulness, good friendship, and balanced livelihood.

These accomplishments are very important for any kind of life, lay or monastic. The Buddha gave especially good advice for lay people in this discourse. If someone cultivates these accomplishments in this life, they will be very comfortable and live at ease. Not only that, they can even attain wisdom and be liberated from all afflictions. Therefore, for a peaceful, comfortable, healthy and wealthy life, we need to realize these four accomplishments.

Persistent effort means maintaining courage and determination to do well and to be good. According to the *Karaniyametta Sutta*, also, whoever is willing to achieve a state of calm should act on these qualities. Not only that, but we will need to maintain this effort our whole life as it will help us maintain our happiness within. Making this effort means we won't be discouraged by sunshine, rain, cold, thirst, hunger, or sleepiness. These conditions will not cause us to postpone any of our activities or any work in our life. Generally, people enjoy getting things by what seems like good fortune or a lucky break, without putting in any effort. Buddha had no regard for that kind of behavior. There are two examples in Buddhist literature of such situations. During the Buddha's time there was a very rich merchant named Mahadana. After his death, his son received his entire heritage but didn't know how to manage it. He squandered all his wealth and ended up living on the street as a beggar. Clearly, he had not made an effort to learn good management skills. He came by his heritage according to his destiny but was unable to protect all that wealth. Again, during the

Buddha's time there was man named Kumbaghosaka. His father was the richest person in the city but ran into some trouble, so he advised his son to flee the city, which he did. He went to another place where he encountered many difficulties and led a very rough life. His father, meanwhile, died. Later Kumbaghosaka came back to his father's city. He went to the palace to seek work and was given the job of city timekeeper. One day, the king recognized him and Kumbaghosaka was able to prove his identity as the son of the former rich merchant. Finally he regained all of his father's wealth. When we compare these two stories, the value of persistent effort becomes clear.

Watchfulness protects our gains. We can gain wealth through effort, and then we have to manage all that wealth and not squander in unnecessary ways. We earn wealth to use for our comfort; therefore, we should take care to protect our assets. The Buddha never approved of spending money on unnecessary things. Management skills are what you need for your life in general – this includes not wasting time in the company of intemperate friends, not hanging about aimlessly, not indulging in too many dances or parties, not engaging in sexual misconduct, and not using drugs and alcohol. All these are ways to destroy your wealth. Leading such a lifestyle will definitely waste our wealth; there is no doubt about that. Therefore, besides having right livelihood and putting in good effort, we must also take care to protect whatever wealth we earn. Watchfulness is a quality that we have to maintain our whole life. From this, we can open up a path for happiness.

We all need good friends and as a Buddhist we need wholesome good friends. The Buddha appreciated having good friends. Good friends are people who are like our shadow, a shadow that never leaves us whether in happy or unhappy times, in any situation. In the *Singhalovada* Discourse, the Buddha spoke of good friends and bad friends. Bad friends always come to us to get something from us. When we are facing difficulties, they are not there for us. They choose to ignore us when we are in trouble. Also, if we don't have something they want, they don't come to us. Good friends always come to us to help us. They protect and help us, and stay with us through any difficulties. We need to have these kinds of good friends because we are social beings and we like living together with others, not alone. Your friends include your wife, your husband, your parents, your children, your brothers and sisters, relatives, or other people beside your family. According to the Buddha's word, confidence creates great kinship. Good friends are those friends who have confidence in us. There is a story related to Buddha's previous lifetime: in a previous life, the Buddha was born as a layperson whose name was Jhotipala. He had a good friend named Gatikhara. At that time, Jhotipala was not a follower of the Buddha. One day, Buddha visited their village. His friend Gatikhara invited Jhotipala to go with him to hear Buddha's teaching but Jhotipala refused. The next day, again, his friend Gatikhara invited him and again he refused. The third time, Gatikhara came to Jhotipala's house and addressed his friend: "Jhotipala, you have to come with me to hear the Buddha!" Gatikhara took his friend by the arm and introduced his friend Jhotipala to the Buddha. "Bhante, this is my very good friend, but he didn't want to come to see you. He came with me today because I insisted." Because of that incident, Jhotipala once again began to cultivate Buddhist practice. Because of his good friend, he changed his lifestyle. He started to practice as a bodhisattva.

Balanced livelihood is very important in lay life. If people don't adjust their lifestyle according to their income, they may face serious difficulties. Buddha never approved of living beyond one's means. If you incur debts, you can't be happy; and you won't be able to enjoy peaceful thoughts because you will always be living with worry. Therefore, you have to keep within an affordable lifestyle. In this way, by earning through effort, protecting wealth through watchfulness, having good friends and not keeping bad friends, we can manage our life and be clear about what to do and not to do. For example, consider a tank of water - there is a limit to how much it can hold. Once it is filled to capacity, it can't collect any more. We shouldn't just fill the tank with water without also consuming it. We fill the tank to consume the water, not to keep it and have it evaporate. Yet we must use the water in necessary, not wasteful, ways.

The Buddha advised dividing one's income into four parts. One part should be used to obtain basic needs such as food, clothing, shelter, and medicine. Two parts should be used for investment. Investment here means work related expenses, for example, travel to work, and also some social engagement expenses. Various obligations such as paying government taxes and paying bills are also considered investments. The remaining portion should be saved, because there will inevitably be downturns in life. During such situations, we can use that money saved for relief.

If lay people can maintain this kind of lifestyle, they will be able to continue living happily and fulfill their duties. They may have opportunities to practice generosity, meditation, and also observe precepts. Such a lifestyle will automatically reduce stress, anxiety and depression. Their life will become very simple and humble and therefore they will sleep well. Their worries will lessen. This lifestyle is called the *Dhammacari* lifestyle, that is, living according to *Dhamma*.

6

KAMMA AND HOW IT AFFECTS US

According to the Buddha's explanation, kamma refers to intentional actions, volitional activities. It means that when we do something or say something intentionally, we accumulate wholesome or unwholesome kamma. It is a process of action, energy and force. Buddha once explained to his monks, "I would like to say that thought is kamma. First we have thoughts, then we say and do things according to those thoughts." We accumulate kamma by using our body, our mind, and our speech. Our kamma belongs to us, this is important for us to remember. My kamma does not belong to anybody else. I am heir to my actions, I was born as a result of my previous actions, and my life is dependent on my actions. My actions are my connections; I am related through my actions. My past and present actions will have a direct impact on my future. My own deeds, words and thoughts produce my happiness as well as the miseries I face. Whatever wholesome or unwholesome kamma I have accumulated, I have to live under the effect of that kamma.

Here is an analogy to help you understand: you can see that the power is on and the air conditioner is running. There is the switch, and here is the air conditioning unit. When the switch is on, the machine will work if it is plugged in. If there's no electricity, we won't get any power, and we won't be able to run the air conditioner. We have the machines and the lines, power cords and switches, but it all needs power to work. Without electricity, there's no power and we can't run any of these machines. Kamma is also like that. There is no simple translation for kamma. We could explain kamma as energy, or as a power, but these words are not adequate translations for kamma because we can measure energy and power but we can't measure kamma. Kamma produces results, and those results generate more kamma. This is the way rebirth comes about, and this is the way the world continues. According to this explanation, causes change into results, and results in turn will become causes, and so on. We are born into this world as human beings, as ordinary people, and whatever we do will keep on building our collection of good kamma and bad kamma. What do we take with us when we die? According to Buddhist teaching, only the kamma we are holding from this life. Right now we are collecting kamma, and when we leave this life we take that with us to our next life, which will be determined by that accumulated kamma. While we live in society, we accumulate much kamma, both good and bad. Our next life will be influenced by the last thought we have in this life. Therefore, our last conscious moment is a crucial factor in determining our next life. After that, all the rest of our kamma follows us.

One day, a young person came to see the Buddha. He asked about the diversity of human society. "Bhante, I can see some people are very wise, some are not so wise, and some are foolish. Some are very attractive, some are not so attractive, and some are very ugly. Some livelong lives, some enjoy average life, and some die very early in the womb. Some live in luxury, some in reasonable comfort, and some others live in dreadful poverty. What is the reason for this?" The Buddha answered him, "Dear friends, this is their own kamma." We meet all these differences according to our kamma. Kamma follows the doer of the action. My kamma is not your kamma, your kamma is not my kamma. There is no Buddhist kamma, Christian kamma, Muslim kamma, Jewish kamma, etc. Kamma is unique for each living being.

Kamma can be classified into four categories according to its relative strength. *Garuka kamma* refers to very powerful mortal kamma, both wholesome and unwholesome. Because of its strength, is can be viewed as the leader of the pack. *Āsanna kamma* refers to what a person performs or remembers in his or her last moment before death. *Ācinna kamma* refers to habitual kamma, what we accumulate in habit over a long period of time, both wholesome and unwholesome. It can also be a single action that is recollected constantly. *Kaṭattā kamma* refers to very simple, unspecified actions that we did, good or bad, helpful or unhelpful, done and soon forgotten.

Kamma can also be categorized according to the way it functions and its effects. *Janaka kamma* refers to reproductive kamma that produces a new existence and begins at the moment of conception and continues for the life of a person. It may be a happy birth or an unhappy birth. *Upatthambhaka kamma* refers to kamma that helps support and maintain the *janaka kamma* that a person receives at birth. If you are born as a human being, with a comfortable life, it is because of wholesome *upatthambhaka kamma* previously done. In turn, if one has accumulated unwholesome upatthambhaka kamma, it will prevent a person from enjoying a comfortable birth and a good life. *Upapīlaka kamma* refers to obstructive kamma that weakens and does not help us maintain whatever birth we received according to *janaka kamma*. Then there is *upagāthaka kamma*, which completely changes our situation. It destroys the *janaka kamma* we got at birth and produces its own effect. We may have been born in a good place or comfortable conditions, but the *upagāthaka* may change it into an uncomfortable or unhappy situation, or the person may die suddenly. Some people have a human birth but cannot maintain that life. After a short time, they die and are born in another realm - a complete change.

Kamma can also divided into four categories according to the time period in which it takes effect. *Ditthadhamma vedaniya kamma* has immediate effect; in other words, we receive the result in this very life. *Upapachcha vedaniya kamma* becomes effective in our next life. *Aparapariya vedaniya kamma* has indefinite effect. It can produce its effect during any life in a person's *samsaric* journey. *Ahosi kamma* is neutral *kamma*. If, for example, an occasion doesn't arise for *ditthadhamma vedaniya kamma* to affect a person in his or her lifetime, its effectiveness simply ends. The same applies to the second and third categories. If an occasion doesn't arise during those time periods for it to take effect, that kamma will become not effective

Buddha advised us not to depend on kamma, because as human beings, we have a very powerful organ, which we call mind. We have the ability to think deeply and widely, thus humans are beings that can change their destiny. Buddha always encouraged us to reach our goal using courage and determination, without depending on our destiny. Therefore, Buddhists do not depend on kamma to achieve their goals. Practicing generosity, observing precepts, and practicing meditation can help Buddhists to change their destiny. Effort and intelligence are the chief factors that affect the impact of kamma and the direction of our lives. Relying on a superpower to influence and intervene in the course of our lives by granting rewards and administering punishment is not the Buddha's way. Our pain and happiness result from our own volitional thoughts, words and deeds.

7

DISTINGUISHING GOOD FROM BAD

Human beings are considered the most important beings in the animal kingdom. Among the animals, humans are gifted with the ability to acquire complex skills and gain specializations. Their evolutionary success is primarily due to their larger brain. The power to think deeply and widely puts them in this very special situation. All animals, eat, sleep, experience fear, and reproduce, but humans can be distinguished from the other animals because of their culture, social norms, values, laws and rituals. People using their minds have created all our social cultures. They have also created many tools. All these tools, from a nail to an airplane, are created by the human mind. All these instruments belong to human culture. There are no animals that create such complex instruments. Humans are changing their behavior very quickly. Some of the food items, types of houses, the kinds of medicines and clothes we used a hundred years ago are no longer in use today. Things have changed in both quantity and quality. Yet today's animals live much the same way as past generations that lived a hundred years ago. Not much has changed in their life, with the exception of domestic animals, and others that are now extinct due to the impact of human activity.

The cultures of modern humans require that they follow prescribed norms and values, and also taboos. There is some form of law and order. All these things were decided with the emergence of the particular society. Therefore, good and bad, what to do and not to do, what to accept or reject, all these were decided by the culture. Generally, we humans share a human culture that is universal. We also have distinct cultures according to ethnicity, country, class, and country, and region. Something that is accepted as good in one culture may be bad in another culture. One culture will accept something while another culture will reject that same thing. This is the diversity of human society that comes about due to diverse cultures. According to how a society's values and norms measure up, we evaluate whether it is a developed society or not. Religion is an important social aspect in the human world. Religions help to maintain a stable society. Taboos, norms and values are always transmitted through the religion, although human elaboration is generally required in detailed religious legal systems. In most of today's nation states, laws are now made, recognized, and enforced by civil authorities.

We find that humans have more power to decide their way of life than any other living beings. We also recognize that all human beings share some universally similar cultural values. Killing, stealing, lying, unlawful sex, and harmful intoxication are actions that are universally unacceptable.

It is possible to formulate a simple method for understanding how to distinguish good and bad. First, if there is some action the outcome of which is harmful to myself or harmful to others, or harmful to both, that is a bad action. From a positive perspective, if there is some action useful to myself, or useful to others, or useful to both others, and myself that is a good action. This is the formula for understanding what is good or bad. It is unique. It belongs to natural law, not to any particular religion or any culture. According to this formula we can understand that killing, stealing, unlawful sex, and using drugs and intoxicants are not good, because all these activities are harmful to other living beings. Those activities are dangerous, unlawful, unwholesome activities, of no good value. Using this knowledge together with courage and determination, people can live peaceful lives, create peaceful communities, and be happy in this world.

The Buddha gave us a wonderful simile to explain human duties and obligations: as irrigators lead the waters, fletchers bend the shafts, carpenters bend the wood, so too the wise control themselves. The story behind this is that a young novice was accompanying his teacher on his alms rounds and noticed irrigators, fletchers, and carpenters at work and thought to himself, if inanimate things could be so controlled, why could he not control his own mind? He retired to his cell, meditated, and attained perfect wisdom while he was still a boy. Farmers need water for cultivation. They get water from the river using canals. Fletchers use shafts to make their arrows, carpenters use wood to make furniture, and in the same way humans can maintain good behavior using their mind to benefit everybody, others as well as themselves.

As human beings we have many skills. We are even capable of destroying this world within a very short period of time. Our common human culture does not permit such a monstrous and unwholesome activity as destroying the world. Our obligations and duties are to do good, to be good, and to live according to the best human qualities. We are supposed to develop our humanity; we do not have the privilege of degrading our human qualities. Nor are we supposed to engage in unlawful activities. Living according to natural law, we have the obligation to develop humanity wisely. That is the path for peace.

8

MERIT (PUÑÑA) AND MORALLY GOOD ACTION (KUSALA)

According to the Pali canon commentary, *puñña*, or merit, refers to calmness, peacefulness, and happiness in the mind. If we want to sustain happy thoughts conscientiously, we need to avoid unwholesome thoughts occupying our mind. Unwholesome thoughts arise from seeds of desire, hatred and ignorance. These are the roots of our unwholesome activity, without merit *(apuñña)*, and immoral *(akusla)*. With these roots present in mind, a person will not experience happiness or calm; instead they will live with stress, anxiety or depression. *Puñña,* or merit, refers to that which helps us purify our mind. When the mind is free of all unwholesome roots, it is bright. This is a characteristic of merit. Another way to put it is to say that whatever helps us have happy thoughts is merit.

Kusala, meaning meritorious or morally good, refers to wholesome skills that eliminate unwholesome roots from the mind. Similarly, eliminating unwholesome thoughts is meritorious and morally good action, *kusala.* According to Buddhist psychology *(Abhidhamma),* we have one thousand five hundred defilements in our mind. Any of these defilements will arise from time to time in an ordinary person's mind. If we develop the courage and determination to eliminate these defilements, gradually controlling and reducing them, we will eventually be able to eliminate them. Even though we may manage to control our defilements, they will arise again and again. We might do good things, morally good actions, controlling those defilements, but sometimes when we intend doing good things, we get discouraged before we finished the job. When we reduce our defilements, we find we have new opportunities to do more morally good actions. There are many opportunities to develop our humanity. However, we still are not able to eliminate them all, therefore, sometimes defilements will arise in our mind again. When we finally succeed in eliminating the defilements, our mind will be completely free and bright. They will never arise in our mind again. A person who is able to eliminate all defilements attains the level of sainthood, and becomes an arahant. They will not return to a mundane state again. There are four states of Buddhist discipleship: stream-enterer or seven times returner *(sotāpanna)*, once-returner *(sakadāgāmī)*, the non-returner *(anāgāmī)*, and the arahant.

To reduce unwholesome thoughts and to develop morally good action, we need merit. Therefore, merit and morally good action have a very close connection. When somebody observes precepts, and also protects and continues to uphold all precepts, those are skillful and morally good actions. When they maintain those morally good actions or *kusala*, they will be able to be happy. This comes from avoiding unwholesome action and not doing anything wrong. The happiness arises because of the merit of the morally good action. Morally good actions or *kusala* help us to cause happy thoughts to arise in our mind, therefore, *kusala* or morally good action is a cause. Merit is the result of that cause. Buddhist laypersons have to live according to five precepts. They are not to kill any living being, not to steal anything that wasn't given, not to engage in sexual misconduct or adultery, not to lie, and not to use drugs, alcohol or intoxicants. These are the basic things that Buddhist lay persons need to observe in everyday life. All these observances belong to morally good actions. Consequently, as a result of observing precepts, we can be happy ourselves, we can live a peaceful life, and people in our social circle will also start to appreciate our lifestyle because it is a lifestyle that harms no one. People will compliment us; people will acknowledge and respect us. These are merits. In this way, the accumulation of merit helps us to continue the *samsaric* journey with some comfort. Moral action or *kusala kamma*, is direct action to stop the samsaric journey, which means coming to realize our true nature. We need merit because we are not yet perfected. We have yet to fulfill the ten perfections to eliminate our defilements. To practice the ten perfections *(pāramī)*, we need merit. The ten perfections are dāna, generosity; *sīla*, morality; *nekkhamma*, renunciation; *paññā*, insight; vīriya, effort; *khanti*, patience; *sacca,* truthfulness; *adhiṭṭhāna,* determination; *metta,* loving-kindness; and *upekkhā,* equanimity. Once a person has attained the final goal or attained a state of complete happiness, or *nibbana,* they won't need more merit because they will have already eliminated all defilements from their mind.

Merit helps us in our life. Good morals, or *kusala,* help us reduce suffering. This means working to attain enlightenment. A person who attains enlightenment is skillful, clear-minded, without unwholesome thoughts, mindful, and lives without any attachment. He or she will not engage in any unwholesome activities. A person who is full of merits only, but does not act skillfully, will still live as a worldly person, with attachment, desire, and other defilements. Because they do not perform morally good actions, they don't experience happiness. A person who is full of *kusala*, on the other hand, has high tolerance for setbacks; he doesn't react negatively to insults from others, and isn't affected by others' influences. He doesn't become upset, worried, or immoral.

Kusala is the activity that once done, is over with, finished. It cannot be changed or transformed. *Punna* is the result and can be developed and cultivated. When someone observes the precepts and carries out their life without killing, stealing, adultery, lying and intoxication, and at the same time develops confidence in wholesome activity and maintains excellent mental health, they can be happy. That happiness come through all these actions. These actions are *kusala kamma,* or wholesome activity. As a result, the person does not give rise to anger, fear, greed or hatred, so they are happy.

When you are thinking good things and enjoying good thoughts with a clear mind, that is *punna*, merit. Recollecting unwholesome actions is *apunna,* without merit, and creates fear. Remembering bad actions and dwelling on regret is not good and does not produce happiness. Always think of the good things you have done. This is how to develop *punna.*

9

TAKING LIFE

The five precepts are the basis for a morally disciplined Buddhist life, so the five precepts are introduced as precepts to be permanently observed. The entire Buddhist community developed based on these five precepts. If the community is unable to observe the five precepts, it will not be able to observe the eight, ten, or any other number of precepts that the Buddha delivered to develop moral discipline. Of the five precepts, the first to observe is not killing any living being. This means Buddhist practitioners are not supposed to kill any living being for any reason. There are disadvantages that accompany the act of killing. There are five steps involved in breaking this precept. First, and most obviously, there must be a living being. Secondly, we must understand that it is a living being. We have to have the intention to kill, and lastly, we have to use some kind of technique that will bring about the death of the living being. If these five steps are fulfilled it means an act of killing has taken place.

All living beings are afraid to die. All living beings want to live. None faces death with a happy mind, and none is ready to give up their life with a happy mind. In fact, a person intent on committing suicide may have happy thoughts about killing himself initially, but when the time comes, at the last moment he may regret it and want his life back. This leads us to understand that all living beings want to remain alive, and, therefore, no one has the right to take another's life from them. I want to live my life, and if somebody tries to kill me I will naturally try to prevent it. The same is true of all living beings. They want to keep their life. And if we try to kill living beings, we will accumulate much unwholesome kamma as a result.

Anyone facing a violent death will naturally face the situation with an unhappy mind. Trying to kill an animal or living being gives rise to anger, hatred, and greed in the mind. In the *Dhammapada* we read that if we do something with a wicked mind, it will be the cause of suffering. Therefore, killing any living being will cause us to have a short life, have ill health and bodily pain, or be born in a place full of great suffering or in hell. If somebody kills his or her father, mother or an enlightened being, it is considered mortal kamma or *anantariya kamma*. This means they will definitely find themselves in a very sorrowful situation in their next life. However, during the time of the Buddha, there was a man, Angulimala, who is said to have killed 999 human beings on his master's orders, but having met the Buddha he sincerely repented. The Buddha compassionately understood that Angulimala had been working under his master's orders to kill. Angulimala became a monk and subsequently succeeded in eliminating all unwholesome thoughts from his mind and attained enlightenment. This story can help us understand that if we undertake killing for a particular purpose as Angulimala did, it does not directly impede our goal to attain enlightenment. Although Angulimala killed 999 humans to fulfill his teacher's request, he himself didn't have a compulsion to kill any living beings. When he met the Buddha, under the Buddha's guidance he understood that he was working under wrong views and changed his approach to life. After his enlightenment he started to live as a monk even though he still encountered trouble from others due to unresolved kammic accumulation from his past births. However, because he attained enlightenment, he would not receive another rebirth; thus, Angulimala would not have an opportunity to experience the results of his unwholesome actions. Fortunately, he had not created mortal *kamma*, or *anantariya kamma*, and that is why he was able to attain enlightenment.

The question arises; perhaps, as to who is responsible for destruction of life by modern means such as drones, where the action takes place remotely. Anyone along the line from the inception of the weapon's production to its eventual employment will accumulate unwholesome kamma by engaging in an activity whose intent is to destroy lives. How about the lives lost in traffic accidents as a result of speeding, inattention and carelessness? Clearly, the safety and well being of others is far from the person's mind that causes the fatality. The driver will say he did not intend to cause an accident, but is that really the case? Speeding, texting while driving, driving under the influence of alcohol, barbiturates and other drugs, and road rage are intentional actions. The driver is well aware of the possible consequences but deliberately ignores them.

We can well understand that all living beings want to enjoy their life. When I was a school principal, I was involved with the pupils as a mediator in their fights with each other. I remember, sometimes pupils came to complain when somebody else punched them. Sometimes I called both of them to my office and had them share the same experiences with each other. I said, 'Twist your ear, how does it feel? Do you like it? Oh, you don't like it? Well, he also doesn't like it either, just like you! Likewise, no living being likes being attacked or threatened by anyone else.'

All living beings want freedom. Our experience of life as human beings involves feelings, thoughts, sensations, and perceptions: taking the life of another and preventing their enjoyment of these faculties is strongly prohibited in Buddhism. And further, we should not take pleasure in watching another living being killed or hurt, or show appreciation for such action. Therefore, we are not supposed to give anyone weapons or instruments intended for killing of any kind, not even those used for sporting activities such as fishing or hunting.

Provided somebody observes this precept of not killing, they will be able to maintain a pure mind as a result. Consequently, in this life and the next life they may have a long life. There are specific benefits said to be enjoyed by those who refrain from taking life: they may have a powerful ability to maintain their body in good health; they may have a well-built body; they may be attractive to all living beings; they may give rise to pure actions; they won't be afraid to go anywhere or face any situation; they may never have any dangerous accidents; they may have many good friends; they may not have any difficulties with their health; and they may not experience stress, anxiety or depression.

Finally, we should not give to anyone what we wouldn't like to be given ourselves; not to anyone, not to any living beings. We want to lead a happy and peaceful life; other living beings also want to have a peaceful and happy life, just as we do. All beings want to enjoy a peaceful environment. We must not harm that peaceful environment. Quite the opposite, we have to have courage and determination to actively develop and spread peaceful and happy thoughts. That is our obligation as human beings. It's not only for their good, it is equally for our own good.

10

A BUDDHIST VIEW OF ASSISTED SUICIDE

All living beings have a natural desire to live. This is the nature of the world. This is the case even for plants. There should be no discussion of human suicide because humans can think deeply, and if the issue arises, they should be able to find a solution without resorting to suicide. There can be many solutions for alleviating a person's suffering. Humans are not supposed to stick to only one solution to overcome the problems they face. They can look at the issue from different points of view and make suitable decisions without resorting to suicide.

According to the Buddha's teaching, killing is not a proper human activity. Even hurting someone is an unacceptable behavior. Everybody likes his or her freedom. Everybody likes his or her comfort. If somebody attacks us, it can destroy our peace of mind and the peace of society. Our present life is conditioned by the results of our accumulated *kamma*. We can see our current life circumstances but we can't see the causes. Because of this, we cannot correctly call anything mine, me, or myself. We have this life and this body to take care of, to protect and to nurture. It is not really our possession and does not belong to us. Conventionally, we can say 'this is my body,' but in reality, it is part of the whole stream of life and not a personal belonging. We certainly don't have a right to destroy it or abuse it. That's why, in all civilized society, suicide is prohibited and considered inappropriate. Life functions according to natural phenomena. We can participate in it, support it, develop it and protect it, but we don't have the right to destroy it.

There is the case of Brittany Maynard; a 29-year-old woman diagnosed with stage IV brain cancer. With an estimated six months left to live, she decided to end her life with her doctor's assistance, which is legal in Oregon where she was living. Brittany began a campaign for physician-assisted suicide, and did end her life that way with the support of her family, also. Now, first of all, we have to question how the doctors could say with precision when she would die. I have had personal experience where this kind of doctor's decision proved incorrect. In 2010, one of my friends went to Elmhurst Hospital in New York for surgery on a brain tumor. After his surgery, I was given a pile of papers from the hospital, all of which explained his prognosis. According to those papers, he could live another three to six months. But after his surgery he went back home to a normal life. He went back to work, and began practicing loving–kindness meditation and mindfulness of breathing meditation. He continued working for another two years. He changed the doctor's prognosis. Two years later he again had a tumor and went again to that hospital for surgery. The surgery was performed, and this time the doctor who was caring for my friend was very positive. He said this patient was an unusual patient, determined to battle the illness. After the second surgery also, he came home and went back to work. He worked for another two years. Recently, the same problem arose again, but this time he went to a different hospital. The doctor who did the first two surgeries had retired and he couldn't find him. This time the hospital did an MRI and other scans, and decided to place him in hospice care. They said they couldn't help him anymore, now he was going to die. And then, with the support of his family he moved to another state. He had surgery there. After his surgery he lost his voice and memory. Recently I got a message from his family. He has started talking again a little bit. He can recognize things. This means, this time also, that a few months prior the doctors had decided to place him into hospice, but he outlived even that prognosis. Therefore, we don't need to take the doctor's opinions as final.

I can tell about another experience. One day, late in the evening, one of my friends came to see me because his mother had been hospitalized. The doctors had told him his mother was going to die within 48 hours. He and his family members wanted to perform some spiritual activities, and give her a blessing. That night we gathered together and we practiced loving friendliness meditation, taking her as our object of concentration. 48 hours later she was able to go back home. Six years later, she died at the age of 83. One of my friends told me a similar story: a Dharma teacher was diagnosed with cancer and given roughly a year to live. Being a careful and considerate person, she went about setting all her matters in order and put her house up for sale. The sale went through with the buyer agreeing to wait until her imminent passing to move in. With all her business aspects successfully taken care of, she spent her time meditating and preparing for death. However, she lived for another three years.

Brittany Maynard tried to escape her pain, but that is not the nature of life. Life is suffering. To become wise, we have to develop tolerance and patience. We have to accept all the pain and difficulties as our experience. Pain is giving us a lesson about the nature of the life. We started this life as a result of *kamma*, and we don't have the right to use this opportunity to accumulate unwholesome *kamma.* That is not the way of wisdom. We may become sick or injured as a result of our unwholesome *kamma.* If we find ourselves facing terminal illness, and if we plan to commit suicide because of that situation, it means we will just accumulate more unwholesome *kamma.* When we get sick, we are not supposed to develop anger towards our body. A patient who is angry at his or her own body may decide to destroy it, but that is not going to end the cycle of birth and death. Destroying only the body will not finish this birth and death cycle. We can finish the birth and death cycle only by developing wisdom and eliminating mental impurities. We are just cheating ourselves if we decide to obtain suicide assistance because of our illness. This happens when we are ignorant about the nature of life.

We can take medicine with the help of physicians. Physicians may decide many treatments for our sicknesses – maybe surgery, and painkillers - but the doctor has to do everything with a compassionate mind. We must always consider the motive, the means and the end. For example, when doctors decide to do surgery for their patients, they have to follow very uncomfortable procedures. They have to administer anesthesia, they have to cut the body using a knives and scissors, and all this causes pain. This is the means the surgeon uses to help his patient recover. Even while doing those hurtful things, doctors and their teams maintain compassionate thoughts toward that patient. Eventually, the patient may recover. Now you can see that although the doctors' work was initially caused pain (giving drugs, cutting the patient), they did all these things to help the patient's recovery. They did everything with a compassionate mind. That was their motive. Surgery and painkillers are their means; the patient's recovery is the end result, which is peace, happiness and comfort for everybody. If the doctor decides to give painkillers or some strong drugs, it is to help cure the patient.

Living with extreme pain may seem to make a case for assistance but assisted suicide is an action that goes against natural law. When a person is on the verge of suicide, their mind is clouded with negative thoughts and feelings - of fear, anger and aversion. This is not good. It is better to leave this world with a clear mind, thinking positive thoughts of good deeds done and gratitude for your caretakers and family.

11

DEATH: THE BUDDHIST VIEW

The general concept of death is that it is the cessation of all biological functions, shortly, after which the body of the organism begins to decompose. It is a general fact that people do not enjoy talking about death. When the topic comes up in conversation, people become uncomfortable. In many cultures it is considered especially taboo to mention death on favorable occasions such as birthdays, New Year's Day, in the morning, and when a person is hospitalized. They think it does not bode well. Contemplating death is abhorrent, and there are some people who don't even want to hear the word spoken.

Unfortunately, there are no limits to when death can occur; it may happen any day, at any time. We will have to face leaving our friends, family, and the things we have accumulated in this life. No one can give us an experience of death; it is something we will have to experience for ourselves. As long as we are alive, we will remain ignorant of the experience. Humans have opportunities to control the world in many ways, and one of them is by extending our lifespan, for which we are prepared to spend huge amounts of time and money, going to great lengths to preserve our own life or that of a loved one. As an example, a friend of mine spent fifty million rupees (about $400,000) for his wife's recovery from cancer. Because of our overpowering desire to survive, we will even kill others when we feel threatened, and in order to maintain our lives we kill millions of animals for food every day.

Even when attempting suicide, at the very last moment a person can experience the desire to live instead. I have read hundreds of suicide notes, ninety-five percent of which contained a final cry for help to have their lives back. They started writing those letters saying they were wanted to end their lives, but by the end of the letter they changed the tone and were wishing for their lives back. When it really came to it, they were afraid to die.

“Before long, alas, this body deprived of consciousness, will lie on the earth, discarded like a useless log.” (*Dhammapada,* Citta Vagga 41, tr. Daw Mya Tin.) When the life force, heart and consciousness cease to exist, that is called death. To understand how death occurs, we could take the flame of an oil lamp. There is three circumstances when the flame of an oil lamp will go out: when there is no more oil in the lamp, when the wick has burned away, or when a gust of wind blows it out. Drawing an analogy, the Buddha spoke of death occurring under four different conditions: death occurs when one’s own *kamma* is exhausted, when one’s own life span is exhausted (that is, the span allotted for this particular life), when both *kamma* and life span are exhausted simultaneously, and due to accidental unnatural causes. Buddhists hold these as the four ways that death can occur.

Although death occurs when the life force leaves a body, in Buddhism it does not signify the end of the life force that supported that body. The same life energy, or kamma, will animate a newly conceived body, but the conditions it will encounter will not be the same, so the *kamma* the new body accumulates will develop differently. Death is just the ending of one chapter and the opening of the next chapter immediately following. The two events occur in rapid succession. It takes only a nanosecond for death to take place and for life to take birth again.

In the *Path of Purification,*[8] two kinds of death are described: one is conventional death and the other is final death. Conventional death has two aspects to it: there is moment-to-moment death, which is a subject of meditators, and there is the physical death that all living beings experience that cannot be reversed. In moment-to-moment death you experience life continuing. You survive, you still exist. But in actual fact, body and mind are dying and being renewed every moment. It is not normally apparent to us that repetitive death and renewal cycles are constantly occurring. Our experience is that we continue living, but we need to understand that death is taking place in mind and body every moment. Our body is made up of eight basic elements. They are the earth element, fire element, air, color, taste, smell, and reproductive elements. All of these exist only seventeen nanoseconds, producing new physical forms. Up to this moment, I have died trillions of times. Each of those times, it was a momentary death.

When a person finally dies, the mind leaves the body. This is the important event because it is the main reason a new life begins. The mind is the place where all wholesome and unwholesome energy is accumulated, and its departure from one body is the point of rebirth in another body. In our final moments on the death bed, we may recall some intense action from the past, or we may have a vivid mental image

8 *Path of Purification: Buddhaghosha*

of a past action come to mind, or we may even see an image or symbol of the next life our *kamma* will inhabit.

In the *Maha Tanhasankhaya Discourse,* the Buddha explained that three conditions need to come together at the start a life: a female being ready to conceive, the union of a male and a female, and finally the mental accumulation from a previous life to unite with the physical body created by the union of male and female. This is the starting point of a new life. These three conditions being present, mind will then lead the new body until the day it leaves that body, which is the point of death of that body. Once the mind has departed, the body will lie on the earth like a useless log.

All component things that exist are subject to death. As we are reminded in the Path of Purification, all health ends in sickness, all youth ends in aging, all life ends in death; all worldly existence is procured by birth, haunted by aging, surprised by sickness, and struck down by death. Yet death need not be a fearful occurrence to sincere Buddhists because they are often reminded of the uncertainty of life and the inevitability of death. Death does not occur only in a certain place, or only among a particular ethnicity or class. All living beings are destined to die. Just as we can't declare war on death, and even if we do fight it with everything we have, in the end we will have to accept death.

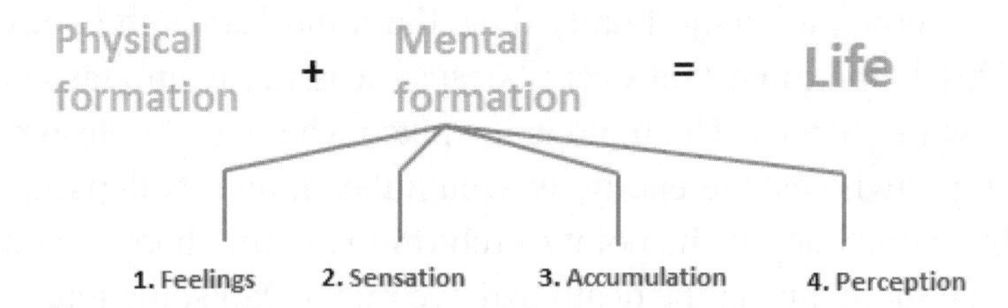

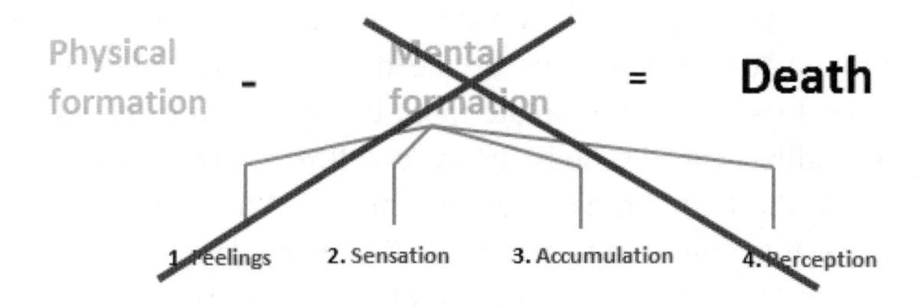

Death is the departure of mental formation

Buddhist meditation is not just for concentration; it is for wisdom as well as concentration. With insight meditation practice, we can take death itself as a meditation object. A person who has experience in meditation and concentration understands what insight is. It is possible to really know what momentary death is, too. You are clearly aware of your heartbeats, palpitations, your nervous vibrations, your sensations changing, your perceptions changing, and your thoughts changing. These changes simply mean momentary death. Once something changes, it will never return. Once a thought moment is dead, that thought moment will never, ever recur. The death of a cell means that when it dies it is finished. That cell can never be revived. It should not remain in the body; it should be discarded or expelled from the body in order to for other cells to grow and develop. Once the cell has died, it must be discarded, just as when the human body dies it must be discarded. The body must be removed from the house and taken somewhere to be buried or cremated so that others can pursue healthy and hygienic lives. This is happening all the time. Through *vipassana*, or insight, meditation, we are able to perceive moment-to-moment death. We can actually experience it, and become fully aware of it. This is one way we can prepare for death.

To practice mediation on death as an object, we go through the mental steps of the decomposition of a dead body. First, we contemplate that after twenty-four hours of no bodily heat, the body starts to sallow. After forty-eight hours, the body starts to excrete fluids. After seventy-two hours, maggots start to emerge. After seven days, the tissues liquefy. Two weeks later the skeleton is visible. When we are in deep contemplation of these stages, we may come to realize nature of the living body, that it is constantly breaking down and being rebuilt. We progress through all stages of the death of the body contemplating several significant aspects, among them, its impermanence and suffering.

How do we prepare for death? According to discourse of *Dhasa Dhamma,* there are ten things to be remembered in daily life. Among them, we need to consider our own death in this way: I am yet not come to death, I cannot avoid death, my life will end with death, all my power and money will melt away in the face of my death. This is not a nihilistic or defeatist exercise; we think in this manner to keep away unwholesome thoughts and actions. Actually, preparing for death can be simple. The Ven. Thich Nguyen Tang suggests that we just behave in a manner, which we know to be responsible, good and positive for ourselves and towards others. He assures us that this leads to calmness, happiness and an outlook that contributes to a calm and controlled mind at the time of death.

According to Buddhist teaching we have to realize our nature, that is, that the nature of all being is death. Life ends in death. Beings fare depending on their deeds, experiencing the results of their wholesome and unskillful deeds. The knowledge that we have to gain is that all conditioned phenomena are impermanent. When we see this with insight-wisdom, we become weary of the lack of happiness. This is the path to purity. There three activities that lead to developing the mind are generosity, moral discipline and meditation. All humans need to practice these to the best of their ability. As a result of such meritorious activity, we develop our own wisdom. In this way we will be able to understand the reality of nature and the world and attain enlightenment. As Buddhists, our life goal is to attain enlightenment, and we must keep up our efforts with daily effort.

From the diagram below we can see the nature of the activities Buddhists have to carry out in their daily life. The main reason to practice them is that a Buddhist knows that because life is so short, our effort to work must be enormous. Even after a person has died, family members assist by performing meritorious activities to share with the departed. Buddhist funeral and commemorative ceremonies are based on these meritorious activities. The family and friends see it as their obligation to perform wholesome activities and share those merits with their departed one. Accordingly, Buddhists observe commemorative services in the name of their friend or family member after seven days, ninety days and annually thereafter.

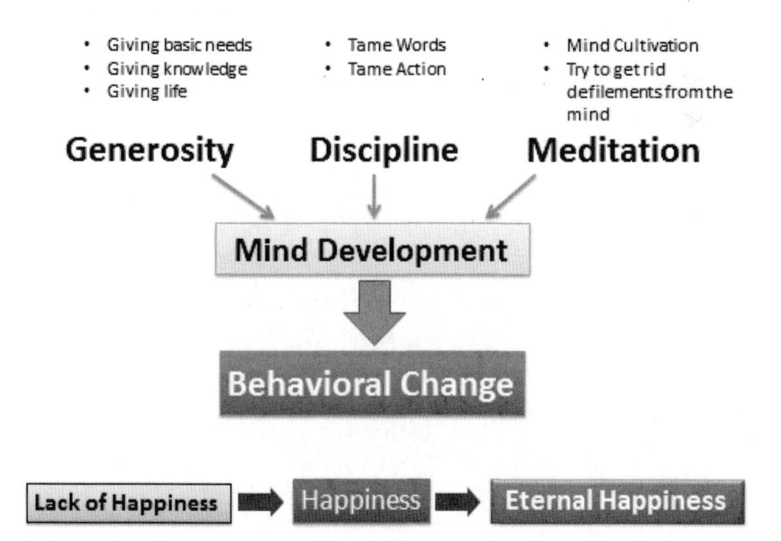

12

MIND, THOUGHTS, AND CONSCIOUSNESS

Do no harm, do good, and control the mind – these are three very important Buddhist principles, forming the essence of all the Buddha's teachings. Accordingly, as Buddhist practitioners, we need to control our mind. We have to tame it. The point is that we need to understand what is wholesome and what is unwholesome, or, simply said, what is good and what is bad. Once we understand good and bad, we are able to avoid unwholesome actions. At the same time, we will gain skill in performing wholesome actions.

Mind is the precursor of all action; mind rules and shapes our actions. We live according to the intentions of the mind. The opening lines of the *Dhammapada,* a collection of the sayings of the Buddha, state: 'Mind is the forerunner of (all evil) states. Mind is chief; mind-made are they. If one speaks or acts with wicked mind, because of that, suffering follows one, even as the wheel follows the hoof of the draught-ox.' (tr. K. Sri Dhammananda). Conversely, the second verse states, 'If one speaks or acts with pure mind, because of that, happiness follows one, and even as one's shadow that never leaves.' Our wholesomeness and our unwholesomeness depend on our mind. If we can maintain a pure mind, it will produce wholesome action. If we don't maintain a pure mind, it produces unwholesome action. For this reason, we humans need to control our mind. Without controlling our mind, it is not easy to live as members of society.

According to the teaching in the *Abhidhamma,* there are 89 different possible states of mind and 52 kinds of thoughts occurring together in various combinations. The appearance of these thoughts, or mental factors, varies according to place, situation and person, creating a diversity of more than 1500 mental accumulations, or mental impurities.

In The *Abhidhamma in Practice,* Dr N.K.G. Mendis explains that mind or consciousness is defined as that which knows or experiences an object. For mind to arise, it must have an object. It occurs as distinct momentary states of consciousness. At the same time that mind arises, thoughts (mental factors) arise also. Together they experience the same object and they leave together when those conditions no longer exist. There are no thoughts without mind, and there is no mind without thoughts.

According to the *Dhammapada,* when the mind leaves the physical body, death occurs. 'Before long, alas, this body, deprived of consciousness, will lie on the earth, discarded like a useless log' (tr. K. Sri Dhammananda). Here, 'consciousness' means it is not only consciousness that leaves – it means that form, sensation, and consciousness, thoughts and mind all leave together. Alternately, when the physical body and mental formations combine with past intentional actions, a living being occurs.

People often wonder where the mind is located. They may think it's related to the brain, and some think it's related to the heart, but mind is not a physical thing; it is formless. Mind is not the nervous system, but the nervous system functions because of mind. Mind is like energy: no one can see it; no one can touch it. It is not subject to the physical body. Mind is present in seven common situations: touch, feeling, perception, volition, concentration, existence, and attention. These are universal activities or aspects of the mind that are common to all consciousness, to all apprehension of an object.

Consciousness is related to the mind and thoughts. Without consciousness we aren't able to perceive objects through our sense organs. We have eyes, ears, nose, tongue and body. Through these sense organs, we have sight, sound, smell, taste, and feelings. Through these sense organs and their objects, we can directly see the physical part of this activity. There may be eyes and an eye object - for example, an apple - but we won't have sight without consciousness. Consciousness supports those physical things, the eyes and the eye object, to give us sight. When we have sight, we have feelings about the object, for example, whether it is ripen, whether it is raw, whether it is good, whether it is bad – we have feelings about that. Then we may have perceptions. Then we may have mental fabrications about that. You may choose to accept them or reject them. Now, you can see, according to Buddhist psychology, we have six consciousness's because we have six senses – the five sense faculties and the mind faculty. The mind can receive both its own mental objects as well as the objects of the five physical senses. These six senses combine with their objects to produce eye consciousness, ear consciousness, nose consciousness, tongue consciousness, body consciousness and mind consciousness. Everything is subject to the mind, but there is mind consciousness. Consciousness is the activity of the mind. In conclusion, we can say that mind, thoughts and consciousness are the same – all these things are dependent on each other and arise together. We use whichever term best describes the aspect of the mental situation we are speaking of - mind, thoughts, or consciousness,

In the Pali language, there are 10 names for the mind to describe its nature and various aspects. To show how descriptive terms alter according to function without affecting the unitary nature of a thing, here is a description of a young man named David. David graduated from university with an engineering degree. When he was in high school, he was famous for athletics and math. In school at that time, his teachers and fellow students called him Math David. When he graduated with an engineering degree, he became Engineer David. When he started work with the Metropolitan Transportation Authority, he was famous among his friends and relatives as MTA David. David is Caucasian, so some of his international friends called him White David. In this way, David's name changed according to his career and social milieu. Mind, likewise, is a single thing. It has different names according to its particular activity in a given situation, and when seen from a particular perspective. Mind is living beings' most powerful aspect and consequently there are many ways to describe its unified activities.

13

MANAGING STRESS AND ANXIETY

Stress and anxiety are very popular words around the world. We may become stressed for many reasons. No one in this world lives without stress. The important thing is, we have to develop the ability to manage our stress. If someone falls in a pit, he will experience stress wanting to get out of it. Because of that, he will use his mind, body, and also whatever aids he can find in his environment to help. He may devise a new technique because of his stress. Another situation is that in today's society, we are very dependent on so many instruments and technological aids that, while being useful to us they complicate our lives and add to our stress.

Stress has led us to invent wonderful things. Think of the earth at night, lit only by the light of the moon. The discovery of the control of fire and its light by early humans allowed them longer hours of activity and security during dark nights. Prior to its discovery, living in the dark was limiting and stressful. This can be viewed as stress management. If we don't learn to manage our stress, it can cause much mental and physical sickness. Medical research shows that heart disease, high blood pressure, gastritis, and diabetes, for example, are directly connected to high stress levels. The reason for this is that those suffering with stress-related illnesses have not discovered how to manage their stress and instead generate positive results.

All Buddha's teachings are methods that focus on managing and reducing stress. If our mind is weak and we do not make any effort to strengthen it, we will always live with stress in a negative way. The result will be that our mind will be filled with negative or unwholesome thoughts. To manage our stress in a positive way, the most important thing we need to know is 'what is the best thing I can do now?' and then do it. 'Now' means in this present moment. We live in this world for a very short period of time. We are born in our society as infants; we grow to be children, teenagers and then young adults. During these periods, there are certain duties we need to fulfill. As a child, we need to develop our basic skills with the help of our parents and other children and adults. As teenagers, we need to engage deeply with our studies and develop our social skills. As young adults, we need to use all the knowledge and experience we have gained to produce goods or services. During this period, we can start a family, we can start earning a living, and then we need to take care of our family members. As human beings, we will have many obligations to fulfill for society, in particular. We will have many responsibilities at this time and we will have to take care of them. In old age we can hand over our responsibilities to the next generation, and we can also change our lifestyle. In following this path, we can manage our stress. This will benefit the whole society. Living as a child with our parents or other adults, we need to use the time for sports and education. That is not the time to get involved with what adults do. The same goes for our years as teenagers. During that time, we need to use every opportunity to increase our abilities. Our teenage years are not a time for adult indulgences. If we use drugs, alcohol or smoking as stress relievers, it will have negative effects on us. We need to manage our stress in positive ways during those years.

As human beings, we need to use our brain, heart, and mind to live peacefully and usefully. We have seen how many disasters and how much destruction is happening around the world due to human activity. Bombings, shootings, traffic accidents, suicides and suicide attempts - these are the results of poor stress management. Because of such incidents, peace disappears from families, societies, and countries. If we develop our ability to manage stress in positive ways, we will be able to put all that energy into creating more comfortable and happier human lives, societies and countries.

As human beings, we have to live according to natural law. No one can avoid natural law. Natural law is clear: when we destroy our living environment, we can expect repercussions. Therefore, living according to the natural law is very important aspect in managing our stress. Nowadays people everywhere are very busy. Why? Mostly to satisfy their ego. Ego is very dangerous thing. Managing our stress in positive ways helps reduce the negative aspects of ego. If we live with a lot of stress, we are not reducing our ego's negative power. There are three simple remedies we can apply to manage our stress and reduce our ego's negative influence. They are generosity, morality and meditation. These are the most important activities we can turn to, to transform our stress in positive ways.

Besides the practice of generosity, morality and meditation, in today's world there are other stress reducing recreational techniques such as walking, yoga, and bike riding. It could be that most of these techniques will help reduce your stress, but there are others those not good management techniques. Think about fishing and hunting, often considered relaxing and stress reducing. Fishing and hunting are not good techniques because they are harmful to other beings. In hunting we use weapons, and by using weapons we spoil the environment. Therefore, those techniques are not good ones to apply in reducing our stress. Conversely, practicing generosity would not be harmful to any living being. If we practice generosity, it will help us to reduce our desire and greed. Less greed and fewer desire means less stress. Imagine you are jealous of your neighbor. When you see or hear them, you increase your stress. Sometimes, even without an obvious reason, you may get stressed. Now take a moment to consider the roots of that stress. It is likely that jealousy, hatred and anger are at the bottom of it. That would be the deeper reason you are experiencing unexplained stress. Without jealousy, anger and hatred, you wouldn't be stressed. In practicing generosity, you get an opportunity to reduce such defilements. Morality also a very important part of human life. We humans need to live according to natural law. By natural law we understand that unwholesome behavior brings harm to others and ourselves. It is universally recognized and understood that behaviors such as killing, stealing, sexual abuse and deceit, lying and cheating, and intoxication are harmful to the fabric of human society. Such behaviors reap negative consequences to us as well as to others. Imagine if the whole of humankind were to live according to natural law – no one would suffer from negative stress. Everybody would have the opportunity to live a happy and peaceful life.

Besides living a moral life, meditation is a very important activity that helps reduce stress. Meditation means developing the mind and learning to cultivate positive thoughts. The effect of meditation practice is a reduction in mental defilements, and consequently, in harmful speech and actions. Anybody can use this technique to reduce stress. If somebody is religious and prays to God, they can do it mindfully. It would be a kind of meditation. If somebody worships God regularly or continuously or pays respect to their religious leaders, they can do it mindfully and it would be another meditation technique. If you are cooking, you can do it mindfully. If you are driving, you can do it mindfully. If you are walking, you can do it mindfully. Besides these examples, there are many other methods for practicing meditation. Meditation on loving-kindness, meditation on mindfulness of breathing, meditation on awareness of death, meditation on thirty-two body parts, and meditation on the awareness of superior human qualities are some other methods among them. *Vipassana,* or insight, meditation is a technique for experienced meditators. The *vipassana,* or insight, meditation technique helps to directly develop wisdom. That is the final goal of *vipassana* meditation. In *vipassana* meditation, we focus on the three characteristic of existence shared by all living beings: suffering, impermanence, and absence of separate being. Insight into these three universal characteristics can alleviate all stress and anxiety.

In today's society, people are vexed about their work. They struggle with time and work. This is the nature of life in a capitalistic environment. They put a value on their time and work. That value is measured with money. We have to find a way to adjust to these circumstances; otherwise we can't live in this society. This means we have to learn to manage our time. Laziness, pleasure, indulgence, sloth and trivial pursuits are barriers to time management. To better manage our time, we clearly need to reduce such mental defilements. Practicing generosity and other wholesome activities will help to reduce these defilements. And we also have to develop positive mental thoughts that will lead to positive actions and habits. Courage, determination, mindfulness, and living a simple lifestyle with few duties are qualities that can help us with time management. Also these qualities are important in managing stress and to have a healthy civil life: politeness, humility, honesty, uprightness, obedience, gentleness, and contentment, living lightly, control of the senses, discretion and respect. Developing a clear mind goes hand in hand with developing these positive qualities. We can lay the foundation for mental clarity by observing morality and practicing meditation.

Competition is another reason for increased stress. Parents tend to compare their children's accomplishments with those of others. They may push their children to do better than others. The result of that is that sometimes they forget about quality while focusing on quantity. There are many exercises we can do to develop our brain. If we don't develop our heart at the same time, we are in trouble. We should develop our heart and mind together. Someone who concentrates on developing the mind exclusively might become wily, and because of his ignorance he focuses only on himself. If it were to his advantage he might go so far as to inflict mass destruction on others, as happens with terrorist leaders. They are prepared to explode bombs anywhere if it is to their advantage. The thing is, that person is developing a brain without a heart, and cannot understand the value of lives. This is the result of competition of education. That educational system can create a skillful person, but that person cannot think deeply and widely about human values. Comparing oneself to another is very unwise. According to the Buddha, no one is equal; each person has their own worth.

My skills are different from others'. I am a different person from others and, consequently, I should not compare myself with others. It is far better that I develop compassionate thoughts, sympathetic joy, and develop good relationships with others. That will help to manage stress and anxiety.

Much of the time we depend on conventional truth, not ultimate or absolute truth. Generally, people give solutions with an eye on the results rather than looking for the cause. This creates more trouble. But if we are able to see things clearly, with a pure mind, it will be easy to find the solution.

14

RECOVERY FROM SUBSTANCE ABUSE

Countless people around the world are addicted to drugs, alcohol or both, and have managed to get clean and stay clean with the help of organizations like Alcoholics Anonymous (AA), Narcotics Anonymous (NA) and other thousands of residential (inpatient) and outpatient clinics devoted to treating addiction. In present practice, most recovery programs think in terms of spiritual treatment and cognitive behavioral treatment for their clients. Therefore, mindfulness has become a very popular approach and much discussed topic in this field. Of the 23.5 million teenagers and adults addicted to alcohol or drugs, only about 1 in 10 gets treatment, which too often fails to keep them drug-free (Jane E. Brody: effective addiction treatment, well.blogs.nytimes.com/2013/02/04). Some recovery programs are not science-based practices; we need science-based practice precisely to gain long term / permanent recovery from addiction. Most addicted people in the field seek recovery in three ways: making an effort completely on their own, by attending self-help groups and working with a counselor or therapist individually. Mindfulness is now recognized as a scientific method and has become its own practice. When a person is able to maintain mindfulness he or she can make intelligent and spiritual choices. Thus, mindful meditation is a technique that we can use to help substance abuse.

The Buddha said, in the *Discourse of Sigala,* that there are six evil consequences of indulging in intoxicants, which cause obsession and heedlessness:

(i) Loss of wealth,

(ii) Increase of quarrels,

(iii) Susceptibility to disease,

(iv) Earning an evil reputation,

(v) Shameless exposure of body,

(vi) Weakening of intellect.

A clear result of intoxication is that a person damages his dignity and self-esteem, making it impossible to cultivate a happy mind.

Addiction is a result, not the cause; therefore, to achieve recovery, we have to treat the cause. According to the Buddhist theory of mindfulness, there should not be a focus on the need to provide treatment for addiction; instead, we have to treat the actual cause of addiction. Addiction is a suffering; in suffering, we find arising of suffering, cessation of suffering, and the path of cessation *(Dhammachakka pawattana sutta).* We are naturally disposed to become addicted to sense pleasures because we don't realize the natural phenomena behind those pleasurable sensations. The Buddha's teaching is realistic and objective. The Buddha says, with regard to life and enjoyment of sense pleasure, one needs to understand three things: attraction of enjoyment, evil consequence, danger or unsatisfactoriness, and freedom or liberation.

Humans do use alcohol and other relevant drugs for recreation, although generally we know all drugs and alcohol contain addictive chemicals. When someone initially uses an intoxicant, they feel happy and joyful at that moment, they feel attractive, and derive pleasure and satisfaction from the alcohol or drugs. This is enjoyment, which is a fact of experience. When a person is addicted to them, however, they begin engaging in evil actions; they cannot think beyond their desire, and can no longer discriminate between what to do and what not to do. The goal becomes obtaining drugs or alcohol depending on their addiction. When the substance of addiction is obtained, there is enjoyment, happiness, and a feeling of freedom. In this moment a person is blind and deaf, not physically, but mentally. Then they become desirous from the craving, and that produces re-existence and re-becoming, bound up with passionate greed.

We can see that the cause of addiction is greed, one of the chief roots of suffering. Elimination of desire is the result of the mindfulness practice. Generally, someone who is not disposed to develop wisdom cannot eliminate desire or greed from the mind. The addicted patient needs to deliberately direct efforts towards the reduction of desire; otherwise suffering and unhappiness will remain with that person. When a person persists in greed, addiction can arise. Simply put, Buddhist theory of cause and effect states, "When this is, that is - this arises, therefore that arises; when this is not, that is not - this is ceasing, that ceases." This theory is called dependent origination. The world continuously exists according to this formula.

The complete existence process consists of twelve factors:

1. Through misunderstanding suffering, ignorance is conditioned
2. Through ignorance, volitional actions are conditioned
3. Through volitional actions, consciousness is conditioned

4. Through consciousness, mental and physical phenomena are conditioned,
5. Through mental and physical phenomena, the six faculties are conditioned
6. Through the six faculties, contact is conditioned
7. Through contact, sensation is conditioned
8. Through sensation, desire and thirst are conditioned
9. Through desire, clinging is conditioned
10. Through clinging, the process of becoming is conditioned
11. Through the process of becoming, starting again is conditioned
12. Through starting again, decay, lamentation, pain, unhappiness, etc., are conditioned.

This is how unhappiness arises and continues. If we take this formula in its reverse order, we can arrive at the cessation of the process of suffering. Those who are able to maintain mindfulness can experience a cessation of the process, in this particular case, addiction.

To change an unwholesome behavior that someone persists in, the only way is to change the mind and thoughts that person chooses to maintain. The mind is a very powerful thing; its power is immeasurable, and it is more powerful than the physical body.

When the physical formation and the mental formation come together, we experience a life. When the mental formation leaves the physical formation it results in death. From this, we can understand the mind as the leader, mind as the forerunner. We live under the control of the mind. Thus to change a person, we need to change his or her mind.

Without changing their mind, we cannot reliably think about making any other changes.

We can apply mindfulness for substance abuse recovery

Mindfulness is a very popular term around the world. To get the real meaning of mindfulness we need to go the origin of the word. According to Buddhist tradition, Buddha's spoken language was Pali, a Prakrit (vernacular) from northern India, and his original teachings remain in the Pali language. We can assume that Buddha almost certainly spoke Sanskrit, which was the language of the Vedas. The Pali word for mindfulness is sati, Sanskrit *smrti.* According to Buddhist teachings, sati means self-collectedness, powers of reference and retention; it can also mean recollection, or alertness. Right mindfulness is at the heart of Buddha's teaching. When right mindfulness is present, the four noble truths and the other seven elements of the Eightfold Noble Path are also present (Thich Nhat Hanh, The Heart of the Buddha's Teaching, Crown Publishing Group, 1999, pp59, New Jersey). Mindfulness is whole body-and-mind awareness of the present moment. To be mindful is to be fully present, not lost in daydreams, anticipation, indulgences, or worry. Mindfulness also means observing and releasing habits of mind that maintain the illusion of a separate self. This includes dropping the mental habit of judging everything according to whether we like it or not. Being fully mindful means also being fully attentive to everything through our subjective opinions.

There are people who say they are being very mindful and we see them doing something in a very methodical, meticulous way. For example, take the act of taking a bite of food mindfully. One may concentrate on bringing food to mouth, chewing, and swallowing. So one may think, that person eats very mindfully, but he may not be mindful at all. He is doing it in a very concentrated way. He is concentrating on touching food, on bringing food to his mouth, on chewing and on swallowing. It is very easy to confuse mindfulness with concentration. If concentration were mindfulness robbers could rob a bank 'mindfully.' The robber has to have' 'mindfulness' of everything: fear conditions; of being aware of dangers and cameras, witnesses, and concern about leaving fingerprints and other biological evidence.

An article in the Huffington Post, 'Mindfulness-Based Relapse Prevention Holds Promise for Treating Addiction,' (11/18/2015) reports that the treatment protocol targets the very roots of addictive behavior.

> Research on mindfulness-based relapse prevention, an eight-week program developed at the University of Washington, offers hope even for addictions with the lowest recovery rates, such as opiate and crack cocaine addiction.
>
> Modeled after mindfulness-based cognitive therapy for depression and mindfulness-based stress reduction, MBRP tackles the very roots of addictive behavior by targeting two of the main predictors of relapse: negative emotions and cravings. Treatment centers, prisons and Veterans Affairs centers across the country have implemented the program.
>
> While the treatment is still relatively young and more research is needed to determine its long-term efficacy for various types of substance abuse, the results so far look promising. Compared to people in traditional 12-step relapse prevention programs, those in MBRP programs for substance use and

heavy drinking experienced a significantly lower risk of relapse, a 2014 study published in JAMA Psychiatry found. Even people who did relapse reported significantly fewer days of substance use and heavy drinking at six-month and one-year follow-ups (http://www.huffingtonpost.com/entry/mindfulness-based-relapse-prevention-interview_us_5645fd24e4b08cda3488638b).

The article includes an interview with Dr. Sarah Bowen, a clinical psychologist at Pacific University in Oregon. She explains how mindfulness works to short-circuit addictive behaviors:

> "There's a shift in the individual's relationship to discomfort. Let's say someone is feeling depressed, or sad, lonely or bored — something that tends to trigger craving and then substance use. These practices are teaching people to notice that arising, and to relate to that differently. So, there seems to be a shift between the experience of emotional discomfort and having that almost automatically lead to substance use. We're seeing a reduction in craving, and also a reduction in the tendency to reach for something in order to feel better.
>
> "Additionally, from what I see and experience, it's helping people become really aware of what's happening in their minds. Once they see that, they have a choice and they have some freedom. We're trying to teach people to become experts on themselves so they can see these processes unfolding and how they lead to places they don't want to go. Then, they see the places where they can intervene."

Jon Kabat-Zinn says, “There’s much more right with you than wrong with you.” That is something we all need to see and understand. Mindfulness Based Relapse Prevention is giving addicts the tools and opportunity to recover without relapse. “Compared to people in traditional 12-step relapse prevention programs, those in MBRP programs for substance use and heavy drinking experienced a significantly lower risk of relapse, a 2014 study published in JAMA Psychiatry found. Even people who did relapse reported significantly fewer days of substance use and heavy drinking at six-month and one-year follow-ups” (JAMA Psychiatry. 2014; 71(5): 547-556. doi: 10.1001/jamapsychiatry.203.4546).

15

THE PATH TO PEACE THROUGH BUDDHISM

Today the whole world is faced with multifaceted and complex problems relating to people's patterns of behavior. All over the world we witness amazing progress in technology. We are constantly striving and working for a better world and increased happiness. Medical science is taking rapid strides in improving the quality of health services. However, the desire to seek happiness, progress in technology and other social advances alone cannot help people to live a contented and happy life unless there is a corresponding mental uplift. This is an essential component to fostering peace and harmony among people.

Conflict exists in various ways and locations in the world. It is a never-ending problem, not only among human beings but also in the animal world. We must all work together to eliminate, or at least minimize, the impact of these problems. Human beings are always in an advantageous position to find far reaching solutions to overcome this threat. This is because they are gifted with an invisible power that is called the mind. I would like to quote the *Dhammapada*.

> "The mind is the forerunner of all evil states. Mind is chief; mind made are they. If one speaks or acts with

a wicked mind, because of that, suffering follows one, even as the wheel follows the hoof of the draught-ox" *(Dhammapada: Yamaka Vagga, 1).*

We need to find new ways of restoring and perpetuating the concept of living peacefully together. Harmful desires, hatred and ignorance tend to make a person arrogant and aggressive, which results in fighting, plundering, killing and many other injurious behaviors. Loving kindness, compassion, sympathetic joy and equanimity are the most powerful nonviolent weapons human beings can wield to overcome aggressive confrontations. One must always think rightly and instantly to avoid behavior that could lead to highly confrontational situations. The following short story illustrates the point.

In the Buddha's time there was a monk named Chakkupala who was blind. One day, after the rainy season, he came to the Buddha at Jethavana monastery. Early in the morning on the next day, while Venerable Chakkupala was walking up and down in meditation, he accidentally stepped on some insects. Later, some monks visiting him found the dead insects on the walking meditation pathway. They thought that the insects had been deliberately killed by Venerable Chakkupala and complained to the Buddha. The Buddha explained how Venerable Chakkupala had become an arahant, a perfected person, and surely didn't have any awareness of his unwholesome act. The insects were dead because of Venerable Chakkupala's blindness, not because of any intention.

He had become an arahant at the time he lost his sight. The monks then inquired about Chakkupala's condition. The Buddha revealed the following story to explain the nature of kammic effect. Chakkupala had been an eye physician in one of his past existences. At one time, a woman who had extremely poor vision had come to see him. The lady promised to become his servant together with her children if he could only restore her sight. Although she was soon perfectly cured, she lied and said that she was not, fearing that she and her children would have to become servants. The physician grew steadily angrier and eventually desired to hurt her in order to teach her a lesson as well as enact revenge. He gave her another ointment that caused permanent total blindness.

This episode tells us that harmful thoughts and their inherent consequences can be avoided if one strives to be mindful and act with tolerance. Wisdom and thoughts of loving kindness, compassion, sympathetic joy and equanimity are the keys to avoiding similar harmful situations.

16

GOOD HEALTH IS MOST IMPORTANT

We are born to this world as human beings. We grow up and then we can see things and we can do things, both physical and mental. We all like to enjoy life using our five senses. We like to see beautiful things, hear pleasing voices, smell fine fragrances, taste appetizing foods, feel pleasant bodily sensations, and mentally, we like to enjoy happy thoughts. Often, when we get sick, we can't enjoy some of these qualities. Whether we become mentally or physically sick, both can prevent us from enjoying these sensory pleasures. However, mental sickness has a more powerful effect than physical sickness. If we become mentally sick, it can become a cause for physical sickness also.

In general, people think the body is more powerful than the mind because around the world people who don't develop their minds think body is powerful. But the reality is that the human mind is more powerful than the body. To illustrate this idea, we can take some examples from Buddha's life stories. According to the Buddhist literature, Buddha had cultivated mindfulness his whole life, even before becoming Buddha. During his self-mortification period, he suffered unbelievable body pain, but he never lost his mindfulness, so he continuously stayed with his practice. Just seeing only this story, we can understand that a person who develops his mind can tolerate any body pain. It will not affect his mental health. But if Siddhartha had been mentally ill, he would never have fulfilled his desire to become Buddha.

According to the Buddha's explanation, there are 1,500 defilements that arise in our mind belonging to mental disease. In addition, when somebody becomes mentally ill, they destroy their present life because of their illness. A simple example might be of deceitful people telling lies out of pride or arrogance. This can lead to their destroying their present life and also accumulating unwholesome kamma by their lies, which will affect this life as well as their future life.

People can become intoxicated because of their youth, wealth, power, beauty, and their education. The intoxication can lead them to do unwholesome and unacceptable things, and even inhuman things. Because of those activities, they will no longer be able to enjoy peace and nor will the society they live in. These things happen because of mental illness, and they are dangerous. That is how mental sickness can be more serious than physical sickness.

We are governed by our mind. Our mind is the most powerful part of our being. All our volitional activities are initiated in our mind, therefore we have to guard and maintain good mental health and take intentional measures to live without mental illness. If we clear our mind and recover from mental ill health, we can live well and happily in society, and will keep our distance from bad and unwholesome behavior. We will be able to keep to good, wholesome behavior. A clear mind is calm, and that calm helps us to concentrate. We cannot reach wisdom and understanding without the ability to concentrate. If we don't have peace in our minds, we are not able to see clearly and think deeply and widely.

Here is a story to illustrate the value of a healthy mind. There were two doctors in a certain village, both in private practice. One doctor became angry because the other doctor was more popular among the people of the village. Many more people went to the other doctor for their treatment and for this reason the first doctor became jealous. He saw that doctor as a rival and therefore devised a plan to destroy him. He met with a group of gangsters and arranged a deal with them to kill the doctor, which they carried out. In their investigation, the police discovered these facts and took the doctor into custody. He eventually confessed and was imprisoned. From this story we can see that it was jealousy and greed that caused the doctor to became mentally ill. Because of his jealousy and greed, he destroyed the other doctor and also destroyed himself. That is why becoming mentally ill can be very dangerous.

Here is another story. There was a garment factory manager who married a teacher and had two children. He began an affair with another woman and was determined to marry her. He planned to kill his wife and two children and carried out their murders. Police investigations revealed all this information about him. At his trial he pleaded guilty and he was given a life sentence in prison. Because of his lustful desire, he ruined his whole life. He lost his wife and children and also the object of his desire. He reduced his life from one of joy and promise to one of suffering in prison with hard labor. This situation he created himself because of the unwholesome thoughts entertained in his mind.

Good health was a central concern of the Buddha. The Buddha said ‘Health is the highest gain, contentment is the greatest wealth, the trusted are the best relatives and friends, and enlightenment is the highest bliss.’ (Dhammapada). There was an occasion when one of the

Buddha's disciples, Venerable Girimananda, was severely ill and in great pain. The Buddha sent another disciple to visit Venerable Girimananda with a message of advice. In the discourse he relayed to Venerable Girimananda, the Buddha explained the nature of mental and physical sicknesses, the causes for these sicknesses, and how to recover from them. This could be the oldest document on record to speak about these medical conditions that were common during the Buddha's time where he lived and traveled. He explained,

'This body has many pains, many drawbacks. In this body many kinds of disease arise, such as: seeing-diseases, hearing-diseases, nose-diseases, tongue-diseases, body-diseases, head-diseases, ear-diseases, mouth-diseases, teeth-diseases, cough, asthma, catarrh, fever, aging, stomach-ache, fainting, dysentery, grippe, cholera, leprosy, boils, ringworm, tuberculosis, epilepsy, skin-disease, itch, scab, psoriasis, scabies, jaundice, diabetes, hemorrhoids, fistulas, ulcers; diseases arising from bile, from phlegm, from the wind-property, from combinations of bodily humors, from changes in the weather, from uneven care of the body, from attacks, from the result of kamma; cold, heat, hunger, thirst, defecation, urination.'

To recover from his illness, Buddha advised Venerable Girimananda to be mindful and to contemplate ten specific perceptions, upon which he would be completely cured of his disease. Those were the perception of inconsistency, of absence of a permanent self, of unattractiveness, of disadvantage, of abandonment, of dispassion, of cessation, of distaste for the whole world, of impermanence of all component things, and of mindfulness of in-and-out breathing.

People are ignorant of the reality of this body and the world. Consequently they are prepared to do many coldhearted things. We sometimes find parents who don't understand their children and children who don't understand their parents, teachers who don't understand their students and students who don't understand their teachers. Sometimes people lack confidence in others. Humans commit many crimes - burglaries, robberies, rape, human and animal rights violations, environmental violations, and so on. All these things we do because of mental and physical illness. We can't properly enjoy the benefits of our human life in this world if we are suffering from illness.

17

THE PURPOSE AND BENEFITS OF CHANTING

I am often asked what the purpose and the benefits of chanting are. Traditionally, monks and lay people chant to obtain blessings. Buddhist chanting consists of reciting *suttas*. These are the discourses the Buddha or his senior monks delivered to his disciples thousands of years ago. Besides chanting them, we need to understand the content of those discourses. The discourses delivered by Buddha or other Arahant monks were a teaching to guide people to understand the truth. When we chant, we use some of these *suttas* or discourses. We have maintained this unbroken tradition for more than 2,000 years. In the past, we have witnessed many people being relieved of their sickness by just listening to these discourses. Therefore, chanting by the monks is practiced at all the auspicious times and events in lay life, like first day of school, birthdays, weddings, wedding anniversaries, deaths, death anniversaries, housewarmings, the first day of a job, and so on.

The Buddha delivered all his discourses with compassionate and loving- friendly thoughts. Therefore, all words in these discourses, or *suttas*, are full of compassion and loving-kindness. When we listen to the words, without even knowing the meaning, we can feel some of that compassion and loving-kindness. During the chanting, we can keep silent and use the opportunity to reduce our unwholesome thoughts. The Buddha advised his monks to always hold compassionate and loving thoughts towards their audience when chanting. The audience must have confidence in the Buddha's teaching, and with this attitude both monks and laity can share good energy. Spreading this wholesome energy to the environment, we can both reduce negative energy and increase good or positive energy in the world.

When the monks chant the discourses, they make wishes for the benefit of the laity after the discourse such as, "By the power of all this truth, may you be well, may you be free from suffering." Monks make these wishes and blessings with a compassionate mind and can therefore spread good energy in the environment. There is an instance, during the Buddha's time, of a mother and father who went with their son to visit an ascetic. They paid their respects to the ascetic, and he gave his blessings, "May you have long life." But he didn't say any blessings for the son. The parents wondered why not. The ascetic explained, "This child will not live more than seven days. He is going to die within seven days." They begged him to do something to help their son, but the ascetic said he couldn't do anything. He advised the parents to visit the Buddha. They rushed to see the Buddha, met him, and in the same way they paid their respects to the Buddha. The parents received blessings for a long life, but not the son. They asked the Buddha the reason why he had not given blessings to their son. The Buddha gave the same explanation as the ascetic. The parents then requested that the Buddha do something to help their son. Buddha advised to them to have the monks help by chanting. They invited the monks to come to their house. The monks began their chanting and continued for seven days. On the final day the Buddha also went to the house and gave blessings to the child for a long life. The story goes that he lived for 120 years.

Monks chant the truth with compassionate and loving thoughts. The sound waves of the chanting are full of compassion. When the sound waves make contact with our body, it helps us by giving rise to happy and peaceful thoughts. The result of that is that we can purify our blood and change its circulation in a positive way. When the blood is purified, it brings health to the body. So this is another benefit we obtain from listening to chanting. The sound waves generated by the chanting can bring about physical changes in our surroundings.

Not only that, even during the Buddha's time, when arahant monks got sick, they recovered after listening to chanting. Among such stories are some that are very famous like Girimananda, Mogallana, and Chunda. Even the Buddha, when he got sick, listened to chanting and was also cured.

A few years ago, one of my devotees came to me one evening to say that one of their relatives was dying. Doctors had explained to them that within 48 hours is the relative would die, and if they had any religious duties to perform, this was the time to do so. They came to me to make some offerings, keeping the patient in our intentions. I advised to them to prepare some soft drinks, lights, and flowers to offer to the Buddha. This they did, and we gathered together and recited the precepts. Being in that virtuous environment, we practiced loving-friendliness meditation for the benefit of the dying patient, and we chanted. Two days later I had a phone call from the family to say that the patient had been discharged from the hospital. She went home and lived another six years. I felt that, rather than leaving her to the lifetime she received at her birth, chanting had helped. I have another experience to relate. One of my friends bought a new apartment in an apartment complex that was more than 50 years old. When they moved in, they found they couldn't sleep well. Once they went to sleep, they kept being woken by many sounds. Not only that, they even heard sounds during the daytime from their bathroom and kitchen. It was very upsetting. They invited me to their house and I chanted for them with compassionate and loving thoughts. I spent only one hour there, and the next morning I had a phone call from them saying they had no trouble sleeping that night. And still today, since that chanting, they haven't had any more trouble.

Other than for healing purposes, chanting also serves in daily practice for reciting the Three Refuges and making salutations to the Buddha, Dhamma and Sangha, for reciting the Five Remembrances, for blessings and other common recitations, as well as to help prepare practitioners for deep meditation. Traditional chanting naturally calms the mind and raises present awareness, reverence and care for all beings, especially with the chanting of the Discourse on Loving-kindness. Any recorded chanting played while in traffic is immensely beneficial in calming the mind of the driver. Listening to recordings at bedtime can give the hearer a peaceful night's sleep, and chanting in the room of a dying patient will reassure him or her, and allow them to pass on in peace and security.

18

MINDFULNESS AT TABLE

All living beings need food to live. No one lives without food. Taking food, sleeping, experiencing fear and reproducing – these are four activities common to all living beings, but as humans, we carry out those activities differently from animals. The culture in which we live is a key contributing factor that determines the ways we do the activities listed above. Humans naturally apply norms, values and taboos based on their particular culture. Sharing and consuming food is part of Buddhist culture. We have to eat in order to nourish ourselves and keep healthy. In particular, Buddhist monks have to reflect when they are eating: they look at the food offered and consider, 'I eat this food not for fun, not for pleasure, not for fattening, not for beautification, not to increase my strength. I eat this food only to sustain my ascetic life, and also to end my past and present suffering that comes from hunger.' Once Buddha said, 'The most painful sickness is hunger.' All living beings need food. We have to eat for this reason. When we are eating, we are not supposed to eat thinking of the capacity of our belly, we have to think only of our need and our survival. We have to be thankful to the people who provide the food we are about to eat, and consider how much labor has gone into bringing it to our plate or bowl. We should eat knowing our limit, and eat knowing the reason why we are eating, because health is more important than anything else.

While we are eating, we have to be very calm and not eat in hurry. We have to be mindful of what we are eating. We are not supposed to talk while eating. We must finish chewing and swallow what we have in our mouth before taking another bite or before drinking. We are not supposed to make noises when eating. We are not supposed to look at others' plates. We have to keep some space in our stomach for water. These are some of the things we have to be careful about. The way we eat our meals directly affects our health. If we know our limit, it will help us to maintain a healthy life. In modern society we are faced with many sicknesses like high cholesterol, high blood pressure, obesity, gastritis, diabetes and also heart disease, and these all depend on our food consumption. If we want to be healthy, we have to have healthy dining habits.

In the modern world, many of us are very self-centered and focus mainly on ourselves. Because of that, we fail to think about nature or other living beings. When we go shopping, we look for bargains, trying to get more things with less money, while the vendors are trying to sell us fewer things for more money. This is the mentality of consumers and vendors. Therefore, the restaurants and fast food places where we go for a meal do not always sell good, healthy food. And not only restaurants, even farmers have to grow and raise produce according to market demand. This is why they use hormones and chemicals, and in addition, they modify the genetic properties of the plants. It is difficult to find natural food in the market. All these artificial foods cause health problems, often not recognized until too late. We humans have made all these changes in food production and supply, and now we must face all these difficulties, worries, and health problems that result. This happens to us because of our greed, self-centeredness and ignorance, and now all humans suffer because of these actions. The hidden reason is that we use food as a commercial product. We can't put a value on food. It is really priceless because food is equal to life. Without food, no one can live. As I mentioned, even if we don't want to eat, we have to in order to survive. Humans will do anything to have food in their stomach because without constant replenishment, we get sick.

Our stomach is not a dumpster. We are not supposed to put everything in there, only what we need to maintain a healthy body. Buddhism describes the individual as made up of five components - physical, emotional, and cognitive -that function interdependently, called the five aggregates. One of these is the physical body. To get those five aggregates to function well, they need vitamins, protein, carbohydrate, and fiber; therefore we have to eat thinking about these basic needs. We have a culture of three meals a day plus between-meal snacks. Whether it is dinner time, lunchtime or breakfast time, it doesn't matter, if our body does not need food, we are not supposed to eat. Most of the time people eat because of desire, not because of the body's needs.

Buddhists and vegetarian food

According to the Buddha's teaching, there is no advice on being vegetarian. There was an arrogant monk, whose name was Devadatta. Once he approached the Buddha and asked five special favors. Among the favors he requested was one asking that monks be vegetarian all their lives. Buddha refused to grant any of his requests. This shows that even there, the Buddha didn't discuss a vegetarian or non-vegetarian diet for his disciples. According to Buddhist history, Buddha was offered alms from many different people in different ways. There were farmers, kings, butchers, fishermen, and people of all professions who offered alms to the Buddha. He accepted all their food; he never refused any of their food. Monks are permitted to receive food for survival without being concerned whether it is vegetarian or non-vegetarian. Whatever we eat, whether it is vegetarian or non-vegetarian doesn't matter, the point is to eat mindfully with gratitude.

But logically and scientifically this body is not supposed to eat fish or meat. We can survive with grains, vegetables, fruits, and leaves. If you choose to eat meat or fish, there will be a market ready to supply you. The butcher is prepared to kill animals for us. Personally, I think that if I am not vegetarian, I am indirectly causing the killing of animals by shopping for meat and fish at the market. We know that all living beings want to live a full life. No animal comes to the butcher willingly to sacrifice their life. People kill animals, torturing and stressing them. All livestock know they are going to be killed. When that time comes, their anger, fear, hatred, and all unwholesome feelings increase. Their mind becomes tainted and that directly affects their body. Their minds are spoiled, and also their bodies. Now we know their chemistry has changed completely. When we eat that meat, we eat chemically changed meat and fish, which could harm our body. As Buddhists, if we are non-vegetarian and consume animals' bodies, how can we practice loving-kindness meditation? Therefore, we have to respect the natural law, that is, that all living beings like to have their life, and none are born into this world to be food for somebody. Therefore, to maintain healthy mind and body, if we can be vegetarian, that will definitely help us.

19

EARNING A LIVING

The Buddha said that lay people could experience four joys in worldly life. They can enjoy life when their basic requisites such as food, shelter, clothing, and medical care, are met. These are basic necessities in life. If these basic needs are satisfied, people can live happily and peacefully. In addition, they can enjoy life if they are free of debt. Finally, they will be happy if they follow a wholesome and ethical way of life. To support these enjoyments, they need money. Money is the means, not the goal. Lay people have the obligation of earning a living in a reasonable and responsible way. They should apply universal law to the way they earn their living.

The Buddha gave us two analogies for ways of earning a living. First, we should gather food as a bee does. A bee travels from flower to flower-collecting nectar without harming the flower, and then in the hive the nectar is transformed into honey, step by step. The other analogy the Buddha gave is of the tiny ants who build huge anthills. They cannot build that anthill in a day; they spend a long time laboring at it. They have courage and they work hard to build the anthill. As human beings, we can be mindful of the ants' efforts in completing their work.

We can engage in agriculture, business, banking, manufacturing, transportation, and the service industries to earn our living, but we need to observe universal law while going about it. In particular, in whatever work we do, our goal should not be only to earn money. In the Buddha's teaching, to be good business people, we need to avoid five particular kinds of work above all: we are advised not to sell animals, not to sell meat, not to sell poisons, not to sell weapons, and not to sell human beings. Not only that, in conducting our business, we should not cheat customers with the scales when weighing things out, or deal in counterfeit money. We should conduct business with our customers with a compassionate mind. When providing services, we must not provide those services with an unhappy mind. Lawyers, teachers, doctors, and consultants need to meet their clients and help them with a compassionate mind and kind thoughts. We also need to develop sympathetic joy when we see others' progress and success.

Whatever the business we engage in to earn a living, we need to maintain a peaceful and pure mind at the beginning, in the middle, and at the end. We need to focus on the motive, the means, and the end of our work. For example, a surgeon will have good motives, and although sometimes the means will seem harmful and painful to the patient, the surgeon will carry out the operation with a compassionate mind because it is necessary for a happy end.

Budgeting money is as important as earning it. The Buddha said that the amount that we earn should be divided four ways. One part we are to use for our basic needs. The next two parts we are to use to invest for future benefits, in equipment, insurance, transportation, etc. The remaining part we are to save for emergency use. In addition to this budgeting strategy, when consuming our wealth, we have to avoid extremes. The Buddha used two analogies here. In one story, there is the miser who heaps up money and never spends it for enjoyment, and in the other, a person plucks the whole branch instead of just the piece of fruit. We have to avoid the extremes of parsimony and greed. We should also manage our lives by staying within our means and not depending on excessive or unmanageable credit.

As householders, at the same time as earning money, we should spend it to fulfill our obligations. This may include paying taxes; helping family, relatives and friends have a comfortable life; helping maintain social services in the community, including shelters, food pantries, public parks, temples and sanctuaries; and arranging religious activities such as services for the departed, family members, friends and relatives. We should be generous with those in service occupations, and help our servants and employees so they are happy in their jobs. These are the obligations of people with means.

20

MARRIAGE AND DIVORCE

Under ideal conditions, we are born into a loving family, and later we may choose to create our own family. We wish to create our own family because we desire a partner in life, and in taking a partner we take on a legal convention that we call marriage. We have observed marriage customs for thousands of years. This is peculiar to humans; it is a part of human culture. To enter the state of marriage, we make wedding vows. There are various traditional wedding vows, but they are all based on the same idea and similar meaning. According to these vows, the couple marries to unite their lives, not to divorce.

Divorce is defined as 'a judicial declaration dissolving a marriage in whole or in part, especially one that releases the marriage partners from all matrimonial obligations; any formal separation of husband and wife according to established custom.' Today's media coverage of divorce gives the impression that divorce is a new and modern phenomenon, but this is not true. There is evidence of cases of divorce from long ago in our human history. Jesus was asked, "Is it lawful to divorce one's wife for any cause?" to which his oft quoted response became the foundation of every Christian marriage ceremony. "What God hath joined together, let no man put asunder. Whosoever divorces his wife, except for unchastely, and marries another, commits adultery." Adultery had been forbidden since Moses received the seventh commandment, 'Thou shall not commit adultery'.

However, the ways people divorce have changed over the years. In very early days, divorce was a personal decision, by individuals and not by any process given by a religion or the law. With the rise of Christianity, however the church took control over marriage and divorce. In the early sixteenth century, a landmark event occurred when Henry VIII, King of England, formed his own Church of England in order to dissolve his marriage and obtain a divorce. He had requested permission for a marriage annulment from the Pope, but he was denied. In 1527, he announced he needed to divorce his wife, Catherine. He was in love with Anne Boleyn. By 1532, Henry controlled the clergy and compelled them to acknowledge him as a Head of the Church of England. He married Boleyn a few years later, but later divorced her as well. He had several wives and several divorces.

The Roman Catholic Church continued to forbid the divorce, and the Church of England and other Protestant dominations allowed it only in rare cases. In the sixteenth and seventeenth centuries in England, it was possible for a man get divorced for economic reason. For example, a man could divorce a barren wife in order to marry a mistress who had born him an out-of-wedlock son, thus allowing him to give the son his inheritance. Nonetheless, Christianity's stance was still too strict for many people. Gradually, in Britain and Europe and in the American colonies, the control of marriage and the divorce decision drifted away from the Church and the State, into hands of local authorities. In the eighteenth century this shift of power to local authorities led to substantial differences in the ease of getting a divorce in different locations in the world. This was the beginning of so-called "migratory" divorce. In the eighteenth and nineteenth centuries, couples went to Scotland, for instance, for a stay of forty days to satisfy the residency requirement to obtain a Scottish divorce. Some years ago, in the United States also, people would go to Reno or Mexico to get divorce. After the American Revolution, in 1780s, many states established divorce laws, and it became a civil proceeding in court.

Most countries allow divorce if the couple need it. It is permissible to divorce if they can take care themselves. This in itself is not a problem. The problem follows when difficulties arise that affect a group of people and society as whole. Then it becomes a social problem, a social issue or social ill. It can also be that a group of people views certain events as social problem. When a couple with children divorce, they become co-parents and this creates difficulties for their children, especially for those under five, who can suffer confusion and insecurity and fear that the custodial parent may also leave. According to research and the media, divorce causes increased stress levels, lowered income levels, high legal expenses, and less ability to care for the family adequately resulting in higher levels of neglect. Stress and other results of divorce directly influence the rates of mental illness and suicides. Mental illnesses lead to an increase in crime. There are many reasons why people seek divorce. The most common are unreasonable behavior, infidelity, midlife crisis, financial issues, physical and psychological incompatibility, and emotional abuse.

According to Sigmund Freud, 0-5 years is the most important time frame for children during which they develop their personality. They need both mother and father in order to have positive experiences. Margret Mead, who did research on child rearing, children's personality, and culture among the Arapesh people and the Mundugumor tribe, concluded that parents have the most influence on their child's development. Abraham Maslow ranked human needs in a five-level pyramid in his book, Motivation and Personality. According to Maslow, our basic needs in life are physiological - air, food, drink, shelter, warmth, sex, and sleep. A second level of need concerns safety, such as protection, security, order, law, limits, and stability. A third level concerns love and belonging found in family, affection, relationships, and work group. A fourth level is the need for esteem, such as achievement, status, responsibility, and reputation. At the top is the need for self-actualization, meaning personal growth and fulfillment. Without a stable family, how can children get these needs met from their parents? Newborn babies and children have to get these basic needs from their parents. Secondly, children need love and caring. This is also very important. Without parents, who else is ready to give the love and care that children need from their mother and father?

Our parents facilitated our birth into this world; one day we may be parents ourselves. This is the way life continues in the world. It could be said; mother and father are the creators and protectors of the world. To develop in a healthy way, children need loving friendliness, compassion, sympathetic joy, and equanimity. Our best friends are our parents; they are the people who can give us unconditional love, compassion, and equanimity. They share sympathetic joy with us in our achievements. If the parents can give enough love and caring to each other, there is a chance they will have enough love and caring for their children.

Children in broken families don't have an optimal family life. They have less chance to benefit from family affection, relationship, and working together as a group. Protection, security, order, law, limits, and stability are the things that we can offer our children to develop our moral life as good citizens of the country. We are born to this world to live a good human life; and according to Freud, in order to reduce inappropriate behavior; people need the influence of the super ego, that component of personality acquired from our parents and from society. The healthy family is where we develop superego, because mother and father are our first teachers and guides, as well as being our caretakers. They introduce us to good and bad. They teach us cultural norms, values, taboos, and language. Culture is a human expression passed on from generation to generation. We learned our culture from our parents as they learned it from their parents. If parents don't have a healthy relationship, how will they be able to influence their children in a positive way?

The Buddha taught that parents are like the sun to their children. Just as when the sun rises in the East, the world wakes up because the earth and living beings receive energy from the sun, so when parents give their children energy, children grow and prosper. The Buddha taught that parents show their love and compassion toward their children in five ways: they restrain their children from evil; they encourage them to do good; they train them for a profession, they arrange a suitable marriage and, at the proper time, hand over their inheritance. *(The discourse to Sigala).* By the same token, these five actions can also be considered children's rights. If the family is not a healthy one, parents and their children will not have opportunities to share to these.

At one time, I was working with forty people who were in recovery from drugs and alcohol addiction. I read the intake forms of these young people, who ranged in aged from seventeen to thirty five. Each one came from a broken family. This led me to think that their broken family situation was a contributing factor for them to become addicted to drugs and alcohol. I had the opportunity to interview several of them. A young man of nineteen told to me that he started drinking alcohol when he was nine years old. A boy of seventeen claimed to have started drinking alcohol when he was six years old. Surprised and curious, I started investigating their situations. The seventeen-year old who started to drink alcohol when he was six stated that his parents divorced when he was five. His mother was busy with her boyfriends, and she also consumed alcohol. First he tried some from his mother's bottle, later he began to drink with his friends. When he was twelve he had used marijuana with one of his friends at his home. This young man was sexually abused too. When he was thirteen he started selling drugs to support his own drug habit. The young man stated that he had used all the drugs and alcohol that we talk about in modern society. He had dropped out of school at thirteen, after completing the eighth grade. In the short time since then, at age seventeen he had done many terrible things, such as taking part in robbery, smuggling, and seeking an abortion for one of his girlfriends. As a result of such actions, he had been arrested by the police three times, and had been in jail, but finally, he started a long-term recovery program. Young people who are in recovery programs have already damaged the civil society in which they live, and there is no guarantee that it will not happen again. None of those young people participate in building up the country, nor do they support the economy – instead, they depend on Federal and State welfare assistance to support them. Not only that, law-abiding taxpayers are paying for their recovery and legal issues.

Nowadays there is much talk about the economic crises happening around the world. To prevent such crises, we have to work, and that may mean sacrificing time and knowledge. We need healthy people in society. Healthy young people, especially, are very important. Family breakups often bring mental, emotional, and physical suffering to family members, both parents and children. They become highly stressed and suffer from anxiety; frequently, they become depressed and often addicted to drugs or alcohol.

We enjoy our social connections with family, friends and colleagues, and we are not alone in this - all mammals and many other species do also. Freud recommended talking things over with someone close when we feel stressed. In Eastern cultures, marriage means signing a pact to take care of each other in front of many witnesses. The benefits the marriage pact offers in Asian culture are confidence, prosperity, heart connection, and happiness. A broken family means all these would be lacking in the lives of family members. Many years ago we had an extended family system, and 30-50 years ago it evolved into the nuclear family. Now it is becoming the single parent family. The duties and work requirements haven't changed, in fact, some have increased, resulting in greater child neglect. Also, single parents' stress level increases, which creates unhappiness. In the family, mother and father are like the mason and his assistant who putting up a building. They have to work together, and as a group, otherwise they cannot succeed in their work. Similarly, if mother and father are not on the same track, children may become confused. They may not get enough care, love, and guidance.

We need to have a clear mind in approaching marriage. Mind is the forerunner, mind is the leader. A confused mind drives us to bad and destructive action; which becomes a cause of suffering. A healthy family life will help us to have peaceful and happy mind. We need to consider all this before entering into marriage, to have that kind of family. The Buddha explained how to seek a compatible partner in life. According to his teaching there are four things prospective partners need to understand: similar confidence, similar morals, similar wisdom, and similar generosity *(Patama sanvasa sutta).* As the old saying goes, an ounce of prevention is worth a pound of cure. As human beings, we need to use our minds with practical insight to have a better life.

21

GENDER DIFFERENCE IN BUDDHISM

Monks, nuns, male devotees, and female devotees, all are disciples of the Buddha. As disciples of the Buddha, all of them have the same goal, to eliminate mental defilements. Monks and nuns commit their whole life to practicing the Buddha's teachings and eliminate defilements. As householders, laymen and laywomen practice the Dhamma path, living according to the Buddha's word and helping monastics who are dependent on almsgiving for their needs. Lay followers or monastics, whether they are male or female does not matter. If they are prepared to control, reduce, or eliminate defilements from their mind, any one of them can achieve the final goal of enlightenment. During the Buddha's time, some monks and nuns had different responsibilities and were given different titles, for example, two of his male disciples became leaders of the monks, and two female disciples became leaders of the nuns. In essence, the job was the same. When somebody became enlightened, there was no difference; they were not seen as male or female.

During the Buddha's time, the status of Indian women was very lowly. They had no rights. They had no right to ownership of wealth, nor did they have the right to visit their religious places. They did not even have leadership in their own household. Buddha is the person who started the movement against this discrimination by opening his teachings to women as well as men. However, after the Buddha's death, those who led this dispensation mixed it with some of their culturally traditional ways. Even today, we see instances of gender discrimination in Buddhist tradition, but those are not in the teachings of the Buddha. Those discriminations derive from the local culture.

Due to the influence of Hindu tradition and Asian culture, in some Buddhist countries women do not enjoy equal rights. Consequently, during Buddhist ceremonies they do not have access to the same opportunities as men. For example, in Sri Lanka, women are not allowed to go close to the Great Bodhi Tree in Anuradhapura, and the same is true at Bodh Gaya in India. The irony of this is that it was the nun Sanghamitta Theri, King Asoka's daughter and founder of an order of Buddhist nuns in Sri Lanka, who in 288 BC carried a branch of the Bodhi Tree from Bodh Gaya to be planted Sri Lanka where it is still growing to this day. In Sri Lanka there is also the Temple of the Tooth that contains a tooth relic of the Buddha. According to legend, instructed by her father, King Guhasiva, in the early 4th century AD, Princess Hemamala smuggled the tooth relic onto the island by hiding it in her hair. Yet sometimes, women are not allowed to participate in some ceremonies in the Tooth Relic Temple. All these things happen through the influence of Hinduism or Asian culture. They do not belong to the Buddha's teaching.

The bodhisattva Siddhartha Gotama, having committed to become the Buddha, started practicing the perfections after receiving blessings from his mother. During his entire samsaric journey, his family members, especially his mother and wife, helped him to fulfill the perfections. Buddha mentioned in his Jataka stories how much he got help from his wife and mother to fulfill his perfections. The Buddha was without discrimination against any living beings in his teachings, not just human beings.

In the *Cullavedalla sutta* (Small Fire Discourse), it is told that Bhikkuni Dhammadinna met her previous husband, Visaka, and explained right view to him. Visaka understood right view and attained enlightenment. Then he went to the Buddha and told him how Bhikkuni Dhammadinna had given a good sermon, and the Buddha said that she had explained the Dhamma exactly the same way he would have and, accepted her words. He said 'excellent, excellent' three times. Not only the monks gave *Dhamma* sermons, nuns also did.

A woman's enlightenment is not different from a man's, but in their lives they may have different responsibilities. Such differences in no way limit a woman's ability to follow the Buddha's path with wisdom. Since the time of the Buddha up to the present, women have sought to eliminate suffering by following the Buddha's teachings. Indeed, many have become renowned and sought-after teachers.

Index

A

AA (Alcoholics Anonymous), 69

abandonment, 84

Abhidhamma, 35, 58

abuse, 44
- emotional, 101
- sexual, 64
- substance, 69–70, 74

accidents, dangerous, 42

accumulating, 10, 82

accumulation, 37
- unresolved kammic, 41

Ācinna kamma, 29

actions
- bad, 32, 38
- destructive, 105
- direct, 37
- evil, 71
- five, 103
- good, 32, 35–38
- intense, 51
- intentional, 27, 41, 58
- positive, 66
- pure, 13, 42
- single, 29
- unspecified, 29
- volitional, 71
- wholesome, 15, 58

activities, particular, 60

activities Buddhists, 55

acts, unwholesome, 78

addiction, 69–72, 74
- cause of, 70–71
- crack cocaine, 74

addicts, giving, 76

adultery, 19, 37–38, 100

adults, 62, 69
- young, 62

affection, 102–3

afflictions, 22

age, 45, 104
- old, 62

Agganna sutta, 5

aggregates, five, 93

aggressive confrontations, 78

aging, 52, 84

agriculture, 96

Ahosi kamma, 30

air, 6, 51, 102

air conditioner, 27–28

air conditioning unit, 27

air elements, 6

alas, 50, 58

Alawaka, 11

alcohol, 2, 19, 23, 37, 41, 63, 69–71, 104–5
- consumed, 104

alcohol addiction, 103

Alcoholics Anonymous (AA), 69

alms, 93–94

alms rounds, 33

Ambalattika Rahulowada, 18

American colonies, 100

American Revolution, 101

analogies, 15, 27, 50, 95, 97

anger, 2, 4, 9, 15–16, 18, 38, 40, 46–47, 64, 94
angry expression, 3
Angulimala, 40–41
animal kingdom, 31
animals, 31, 40, 50, 91, 94, 96
  domestic, 31
anthills, 95
anticipation, 73
ants, 95
Anuradhapura, 108
anxiety, 2, 4, 16, 25, 35, 42, 61, 65, 67, 105
Aparapariya vedaniya kamma, 30
apartment, 90
apprehension, 59
arahant, 36, 78
Arapesh, 102
Āsanna kamma, 29
ascetic, 88
ascetic life, 91
Asian culture, 105, 108
Asoka, King, 108
attachment, 10, 13, 37–38
attraction, 70

B

balanced livelihood, 22, 24
barbiturates, 41
BC, 108
beautification, 91
bee, 95
beggar, 3, 22
behavior, 19, 22, 31, 64, 77–78, 103
  addictive, 74–75
  good, 33
  injurious, 78
  unacceptable, 43
  unreasonable, 101
  unwholesome, 64, 72, 82
  wholesome, 82
behaviors reap, 64
beliefs, 1, 4, 7
  false, 13
  form, 7
Believing, 7
between-meal snacks, 93
Bhante, 24, 28
bhikku, 21
bhikkuni, 21
Bhikkuni Dhammadinna, 109
biological evidence, 74
birth, 29–30, 41, 46, 51–52, 89, 102
  comfortable, 29
  happy, 29
  human, 30
  unhappy, 29
birthdays, 49, 87
bite, 73, 92
blessings, 45, 87–90, 108
blind, 71, 78
bliss, highest, 83
blood, 89
blood pressure, high, 61, 92
bloom, 15
  lotuses, 15
Bodh Gaya, 108
bodhisattva, 24
bodhisattva Siddhartha Gotama, 108
body, 10, 27, 42–43, 46, 49–54, 58–59, 61, 70, 81, 84, 89, 93–94
  conceived, 51
  dead, 54
  healthy, 93
  human, 53
  living, 54
  physical, 52, 58–59, 72, 93
  this is my, 44
body-and-mind awareness, 73
body consciousness, 59
body-diseases, 84
body pain, 81–82
Boleyn, Anne, 100
Bombings, 63
Bowen, Sarah, 75

boy, 33, 104
brain, 31, 58, 63, 66
brain tumor, 44
branch, 97, 108
breakfast time, 93
breathing meditation, 44
brightness, 7
Britain, 100
Brittany, 44
Brody, Jane E., 69
broken families, 102, 104–5
broken family situation, 104
Buddha, 1, 4–7, 11, 15, 17–19, 21–25, 27–30, 39–40, 70, 73, 78, 81–84, 87–91, 93–97, 106–9
    becoming, 81
Buddhaghosha, 51
Buddha's death, 108
Buddha's Dhammachakkapavattana Sutta, 21
Buddha's disciples, 21, 84
Buddha's explanation, 27, 82
Buddha's goal, 17
Buddha's guidance, 18, 40
Buddha's life stories, 81
Buddha's path, 109
Buddha's task, 17
Buddha's teaching, 6–7, 17–18, 21, 24, 43, 57, 62, 70, 73, 88, 93, 96, 107–9
Buddha's time, 22–23, 78, 84, 88–89, 107
Buddha's word, 10, 21, 24, 107
Buddhism, 1, 5, 7, 17, 42, 50, 77, 93, 107
Buddhist accounts, 15
Buddhist ceremonies, 108
Buddhist chanting, 87
Buddhist community, 7, 39
Buddhist countries women, 108
Buddhist culture, 91
Buddhist discipleship, 36
Buddhist family, 19
Buddhist funeral and commemorative ceremonies, 55
Buddhist history, 93
Buddhist inquiry, 7
Buddhist kamma, 29
Buddhist laypersons, 37
BUDDHIST LIFE, 17
Buddhist life, living, 19
Buddhist literature, 22, 81
Buddhist meditation, 53
Buddhist monks, 91
Buddhist nuns, 108
Buddhist practice, 24
Buddhist practitioners, 39, 57
Buddhist principles, 57
Buddhist psychology, 35, 59
Buddhists, 3, 5, 7, 9, 11, 15, 18–19, 21, 23, 30, 37, 43, 49–50, 55, 94
    fundamental, 19
    sincere, 52
Buddhists and vegetarian food, 93
Buddhists use confidence, 7
Buddhist teachings, 6, 10–11, 28, 54, 73
Buddhist theory, 71
Buddhist theory of mindfulness, 70
Buddhist tradition, 73, 108
Budgeting money, 96
budgeting strategy, 96
buds, 15
business, 45, 96
butchers, 94

C

calmness, 35, 54
cancer, 45, 50
    stage IV brain, 44
capacity, 25, 91
    perceptive, 2
carbohydrate, 93
care, 23, 43, 45, 62, 90, 101–2, 105
    medical, 95
    uneven, 84
carelessness, 41
caretakers, 47, 103

caring, 44, 102
carpenters, 33
cases, particular, 72
Catherine, 100
Caucasian, 60
cause obsession, 70
cell, 33, 53
cessation, 12, 49, 70, 72, 84
chair, 6
Chakkupala, 78
Chakkupala's condition, 78
change, 7, 28, 30, 62, 72, 89
    complete, 30
chant, 87
chanting, 87–90
    benefits of, 87
    recorded, 90
cheat customers, 96
cheating ourselves, 46
chemicals, 92
    addictive, 71
chief roots, 71
child, 62, 88–89, 105
child rearing, 102
children, 24, 62, 66, 79, 83, 85, 101–3, 105
children divorce, 101
children energy, 103
Children in broken families, 102
children's accomplishments, 66
children's rights, 103
child's development, 102
cholesterol, high, 92
Christianity, 100
Christian kamma, 29
Christian marriage ceremony, 100
Chunda, 89
church, 100
circulation, 89
citizens, good, 103
Citta Vagga, 50
city, 23
    father's, 23
city timekeeper, 23
civil authorities, 32
civil life, healthy, 66
class, 32, 52
classic questions, 6
clients, 69, 96
clinging, 10, 72
clinical psychologist, 75
comfort, 23, 28, 37, 43, 47
comfortable conditions, 30
comfortable life, 29, 97
commandment, 100
commemorative ceremonies, 55
commercial product, 93
commitment, positive, 2
communities, peaceful, 33
community, 7, 39, 97
compassion, 2, 14, 78–79, 87–89, 102–3
competition, 66
component, 52, 77, 84, 103
components, five, 93
comprehending, 9
comprehension, 9
concentration, 2, 11, 13–15, 18, 45, 53, 59, 74
    maintaining, 19
concept, 49, 78
conditioned phenomena, 54
conduct business, 96
confidence, 24, 38, 85, 88, 105–6
Conflict, 77
confrontational situations, 78
connection, close, 36
connections, 27
    social, 105
consciousness, 10, 50, 57–60, 71–72
    ear, 59
    eye, 59
    nose, 59
    tongue, 59
consistency, 2
constant replenishment, 93

consultants, 96
consumables, giving, 2
contact, 10, 72, 89
    sense, 10
contemplation, 2
    deep, 54
contentment, 4, 66, 83
contraction, 5
control, 2, 18, 33, 36, 49, 57–58, 61, 66, 72, 100, 107
    wise, 33
conversation, 49
co-parents, 101
countries, 17, 32, 63, 74, 101, 103–4
couple marries, 99
couples, 101
courage, 2, 9, 11, 13, 30, 33, 36, 42, 66, 95
    maintaining, 22
craving, 71, 74–75
    sensual, 13
creation stories, 5
Creator God, 5, 7
creators, 15, 102
crimes, 85, 101
crises, 104
    economic, 104
Crown Publishing Group, 73
Culamalukya Sutta, 6
Cullavedalla sutta, 109
cultivation, 9, 33
culture, 5, 31–33, 49, 91, 93, 102–3
    distinct, 32
    local, 108
    particular, 91
    social, 31
custodial parent, 101
cycle, 18, 46

D

dangers, 70, 74
dark nights, 61
David, 60
David's name, 60
Daw Mya Tin, 50
days, 15, 54–55, 88–89, 101
    early, 100
death, 7, 9, 22, 29, 39, 45–46, 49–54, 58, 65, 72, 87
    faces, 39
    final, 51
    momentary, 51, 53
    moment-to-moment, 51, 53
    physical, 51
    repetitive, 51
    violent, 40
death anniversaries, 87
death bed, 51
death cycle, 46
debts, 25, 95
decomposition, 54
deeds, 27, 30, 54
    good, 47
    unskillful, 54
defeatist exercise, 54
defilements, 4, 9, 11–15, 36–38, 64, 66, 82, 107
degree, engineering, 60
delusion, 2, 4, 15
depression, 2, 16, 25, 35, 42, 74
descriptive terms, 60
destiny, 22, 30
destruction, 5, 41, 63
    inflict mass, 66
Devadatta, 93
devotees, 89
    female, 107
    male, 107
Dhamma, 7, 21, 25, 90, 109
Dhammacari lifestyle, 25
Dhammachakka pawattana sutta, 70
Dhammapada, 40, 50, 57–58, 77–78, 83
Dhamma path, 107
Dhamma sermons, 109
Dharma teacher, 45
Dhasa Dhamma, 54
diabetes, 62, 84, 92
difficulties, 23–25, 42, 46, 92, 101

dinner time, 93
disasters, 5, 63
natural, 5
disciples, 7, 84, 87, 93, 107
female, 107
male, 107
discipline, 4
ethical, 1
moral, 11, 39, 55
disciplined Buddhist life, 39
discomfort, 75
emotional, 75
discourses, 22, 54, 70, 84, 87–88, 90, 103, 109
discovery, 61
discretion, 4, 66
discrimination, 7, 108–9
gender, 108
disease, 70, 84
mental, 82
dispensation, 7, 108
diversity, 28, 32, 58
divorce, 99–101
migratory, 101
divorce decision, 100
doctors, 44–47, 83, 89, 96
doctor's assistance, 44
doctor's decision, 44
draught-ox, 57, 78
drink alcohol, 104
driver, 41, 90
drugs, 2, 19, 23, 33, 41, 69–71, 103–5
giving, 46
obtaining, 71
strong, 47
duties, 4, 9, 14, 25, 33, 62, 66, 105
human, 33
religious, 89

E

ear-diseases, 84
earning, 25, 70, 95–96
earning money, 97
ears, 10, 41, 59
earth, 6, 50, 52, 58, 61, 103
earth element, 51
earthquakes, 5
Eastern cultures, 105
eat, 31, 91–94
eating fish, 94
eating, 91–92
eating meat, 94
eat thinking, 91, 93
economic reason, 100
education, 62, 66, 82
educational system, 66
effect
indefinite, 30
kammic, 78
negative, 63
powerful, 81
effectiveness, 30
effect states, 71
effort, 12–13, 22–23, 25, 30, 37, 55, 62, 69, 95
daily, 55
good, 23
ego, 14, 63
super, 103
Eightfold Noble Path, 73
electricity, 28
elements
basic, 51
natural, 6, 14
reproductive, 51
Elimination, 71
Elmhurst Hospital in New York for surgery, 44
emergency use, 96
encountered trouble, 41
energy, 27–28, 59, 63, 103
good, 88
measure, 28
negative, 88
positive, 88
unwholesome, 51
wholesome, 88

Engineer David, 60
England, 100
enjoyment, 21, 42, 70–71, 95, 97
enlightenment, 7, 12, 15, 37, 40–41, 55, 83, 107
    attained, 40–41, 109
    woman's, 109
environment, 11, 14, 61, 64, 88
    capitalistic, 65
    living, 63
    peaceful, 42
    virtuous, 18, 89
environmental violations, 85
equanimity, 14, 37, 78–79, 102
ethical practice, 19
ethnicity, 19, 32
    particular, 52
Europe, 100
evening, 45, 89
everyday life, 37
evil, 57, 103
evil consequences, 70
evil reputation, 70
evolutionary success, 31
excrete fluids, 54
expansion, 5
expenses, 25
    high legal, 101
    social engagement, 25
experience, 1, 6, 9, 13, 41–42, 45–46, 49–51, 53, 58, 62, 71–72, 75, 90, 95
experience anger, 14
experience fear, 31
experience happiness, 35, 38
experience life, 51
experience ourselves, 15
experience stress, 42
experience stress wanting, 61
experience wisdom, 2
explication, 15
explode bombs, 66
extinguishing, 9
extremes, 21, 97
eyes, 10, 59, 67

F

factors, 12–13, 28, 71, 91, 104
    chief, 30
    mental, 58
faculties, 10, 42, 72
    five, 10
    five sense, 59
faith, 5, 7
family, 3, 21, 24, 44–45, 47, 49, 55, 62–63, 89, 99, 101–3, 105–6
    healthy, 103
    nuclear, 105
    stable, 102
family breakups, 105
family life, optimal, 102
family members, 45, 55, 62, 97, 105, 108
family system, extended, 105
farmers, 33, 92, 94
father, 23, 40, 88, 101–3, 105, 108
fellow students, 60
female laypersons, 21
fights, 41, 52
fingerprints, 74
fish, 94
fishing, 42, 64
five precepts, 2, 11, 21, 37, 39
    basic, 4
Five Remembrances, 90
flame, 50
fletchers, 33
flowers, 89, 95
    lotus, 15
followers, 1, 24, 107
follow-ups, 75–76
food, 25, 50, 73–74, 91, 93–95, 102
    healthy, 92
    natural, 92
food consumption, 92
food items, 31
food pantries, 97

food production, 92
forerunner, 57, 72, 77, 105
formal separation, 99
formula, 32–33, 71–72
fortune, good, 22
foundation, 11, 66, 99
  spiritual, 15
framework, particular, 1
freedom, 9, 42–43, 70–71, 75
Freud, 103, 105
friend Gatikhara, 24
friend Jhotipala, 24
friends, 3, 24, 29, 44–45, 49–50, 55, 60, 83, 90, 97, 104–5
friendship, good, 22
fruits, 94, 97
fulfillment, 102
  perfect character, 3
functions, 29, 59–60, 93
  biological, 49

G

garment factory manager, 83
Garuka kamma, 29
gastritis, 61, 92
Gatikhara, 24
GENDER DIFFERENCE, 107
generation, 31, 62, 103
generosity, 2, 4, 15, 30, 37, 55, 63–64, 66, 106
genetic properties, 92
Girimananda, 89
girlfriends, 104
goal, 4, 9, 16–18, 30, 40, 71, 95–96, 107
  final, 37, 65, 107
GOAL of BUDDHIST LIFE, 17
God, 1, 4–5, 7, 65
  creative superpower, 1
  worships, 65
God hath, 100
Good morals, 37
gratitude, 4, 47, 94
Great Bodhi Tree, 108
group, 21, 83, 101, 103, 105
  particular, 17
  self-help, 69
Guhasiva, King, 108
guidance, 2–3, 17, 105
guides, 7, 15, 103
guilty, pleaded, 83

H

habits, 10, 29, 66
  drug, 104
  healthy dining, 92
  mental, 73
  releasing, 73
  self-centered, 14
happiness, 4, 21–23, 27, 35–36, 38, 47, 54, 57, 71, 77, 105
  complete, 37
  increased, 77
happiness result, 30
harbors, 11, 15
harmful activities, avoiding, 19
harmful situations, 79
head-diseases, 84
healing purposes, 90
health, 42, 52, 83, 89, 92
  good, 42, 81, 83
health problems, 93
  artificial foods cause, 92
health services, 77
healthy family life, 105
hearing-diseases, 84
heart, 50, 58, 63, 66, 73
heart connection, 105
heart disease, 61, 92
heat, 84
  bodily, 54
heavy drinking, 75–76
heedlessness, 70
helping family, 97
hemorrhoids, 84
Henry, 100

Henry VIII, 100
heritage, 22
Hinduism, 108
Hindu tradition, 108
histories, hidden, 6
history, 6
    human, 99
home, 44–45, 89, 104
hoof, 57, 78
hospice care, 45
hospital, 44–45, 89
hours, 45, 54, 61, 89–90
house, 31, 45, 53, 88–90
householders, 97, 107
housewarmings, 87
Huffington Post, 74
human activity, 5, 31, 43, 63
human beings, 2, 16–17, 28, 30–31, 33, 40, 42, 62–63, 77–78, 81, 95–96, 106, 109
    superior, 3
human beings share, 32
human culture, 31–32, 99
    common, 33
human elaboration, 32
human expression, 103
humanity, 2, 16, 33–34, 36
humankind, 64
human life, 64, 85
    good, 103
human qualities, 33
    best, 33
    superior, 65
humans, 5, 9, 30–33, 40, 43, 49, 55, 58, 64, 70, 85, 91–93, 99
    early, 61
    modern, 32
human society, 28, 32, 64
humans share, 32
human world, 32
humble, 4, 25
humors, bodily, 84
hundred defilements, five, 36
hunger, 22, 84, 91
hurry, 3, 92
hurt, 42, 79
husband, 24, 99, 109

I

ignorance, 15, 18, 35, 66, 71, 78, 93
ill health, 40
    mental, 82
illness, 44, 46, 82, 84–85
    physical, 85
    terminal, 46
images, 10, 52
    mental, 51
immoral, 35, 38
impermanence, 18, 54, 65, 84
impermanent, 54
in-and-out breathing, 84
inattention, 41
incidents, 24, 63
income, 25
inconsistency, 84
India, 7, 108
    northern, 73
Indian women, 107
individuals, 12, 100
individual's relationship, 75
indulgences, 65, 73
    adult, 63
    excessive, 21
indulging, 23, 70
inevitability, 52
influence, negative, 63
inheritance, 100, 103
insects, 78
    dead, 78
insight meditation practice, 53
insight-wisdom, 54
instruments, 31, 42, 61
    complex, 31
intake forms, 103
intelligence, 30

intemperate friends, 23
intentional measures, 82
intentions, 12, 39, 57, 78, 89
    right, 11–12
interdependent existence, 18
international friends, 60
interview, 75, 104
intoxicants, 12, 33, 37, 70–71
intoxication, 38, 64, 70, 82
    harmful, 32
investigator, 17
investments, 25
invisible power, 77
irrigators, 33
    noticed, 33

J

jamapsychiatry, 76
JAMA Psychiatry, 75–76
Jataka stories, 109
jealous, 64, 83
jealousy, 64, 83
Jesus, 99
Jethavana monastery, 78
Jewish kamma, 29
Jhotipala, 24
Jhotipala's house, 24
joys, 83, 95
judicial declaration dissolving, 99

K

Kabat-Zinn, Jon, 76
kamma, 12, 19, 27–30, 50–52
    accumulated, 28, 43
    anantariya, 40–41
    bad, 28
    ditthadhamma vedaniya, 30
    good, 28
    habitual, 29
    janaka, 29–30
    kusala, 37–38
    measure, 28
    neutral, 30
    obstructive, 29
    reproductive, 29
    result of, 46, 84
    translations for, 28
    unwholesome, 27, 40–41, 46, 82
    upagāthaka, 29
Karaniyametta Sutta, 22
Kaṭattā kamma, 29
killing, 2, 19, 32–33, 38–40, 42–43, 64, 78, 94
    act of, 39
kindergarten, 9
kindness meditation, 44
kings, 23, 94, 100
knowledge, 3, 6–7, 12–13, 33, 54, 62, 105
    blissful, 3
    giving, 2
Kumbaghosaka, 23
kusala, 35–38

L

labor, 91
    hard, 83
laity, 88
lamentation, 72
lamp, 50
    oil, 50
lamps unto themselves, 7
landmark event, 100
language, 73, 103
    spoken, 73
law-abiding taxpayers, 104
laws, 31–32, 100, 102–3
    established divorce, 101
    universal, 95–96
Lawyers, 96
layperson, 24
laypersons, male, 21
Laziness, 65
leaders, 1, 7, 29, 72, 105, 107
    religious, 65
    terrorist, 66
legal convention, 99

lesson, 46, 79
letters, 50
level, 36, 101–2
 high stress, 62
 increased stress, 101
 lowered income, 101
liberation, 14, 70
life energy, 50
life force, 50
life functions, 44
life goal, 55
life sentence, 83
lifestyle, 23–25, 37, 62, 66
 calm, 3
 peaceful, 19
lifetime, 14, 24, 30, 89
likes, 43
livelong, 28
livestock, 94
living beings experience, 51
local authorities, 100–101
locations, 77, 101
log, 50, 52, 58
logical perspective, 7
long-term efficacy, 74
long-term recovery program, 104
love, 100, 102–3, 105
 unconditional, 102
loving, 14, 44, 87
loving family, 99
loving friendliness, 14, 102
loving kindness, 14, 78–79
loving-kindness, 37, 65, 87–88, 90
LT, 23, 25, 83, 85
lucky break, 22

M

machines, 28
Mahadana, 22
Maha Tanhasankhaya Discourse, 52
Management skills, 23
 good, 22
market, 92, 94
marriage, 99–100, 103, 105–6
marriage annulment, 100
marriage customs, observed, 99
marriage pact, 105
marriage partners, 99
married Boleyn, 100
marries, 83, 100
Maslow, 102
 Abraham, 102
master's orders, 40
Math David, 60
Maynard, Brittany, 44–45
May you have long life, 88
MBRP, 74
MBRP programs for substance use, 74
MBRP programs for substance use and heavy drinking, 76
Mead, Margret, 102
meals, 92–93
measurable evidence, 7
meat, 94, 96
 changed, 94
media coverage, 99
medical conditions, 84
Medical research, 61
Medical science, 77
medicines, 25, 31, 46
meditation, 2, 4, 11, 15, 18, 25, 30, 53, 55, 63–66, 70, 78
 deep, 90
meditation object, 53
meditation pathway, walking, 78
meditation practice, 65
 strong, 18
meditation technique, 65
meditators, 51, 65
Mendis, 58
mental accumulations, 52, 58
mental afflictions, 18
 reducing, 18
mental clarity, 66

mental connection, 10
mental defilements, 9–11, 65, 107
mental fabrications, 59
mental formations, 10, 58, 72
mental health, 82
  excellent, 38
  good, 82
mental illnesses, 16, 82, 101
mental impurities, 46, 58
mentality, 92
mental situation, 60
mental steps, 54
mental uplift, 77
merchant, rich, 22–23
merit, 35–38
meritorious, 35
meritorious activities, 55
  performing, 55
methods
  best, 4
  scientific, 69
Metropolitan Transportation Authority, 60
Mexico, 101
Middle Way, 10–11, 13
Middle Way activities, 11
midlife crisis, 101
mind, 1–2, 6, 9–15, 18, 30–31, 33, 35–37, 40, 51–52, 57–64, 66, 71–73, 77, 81–83, 105–7
  compassionate, 46–47, 88, 96
  confused, 105
  controlled, 54
  deluded, 10
  healthy, 83, 94
  human, 31, 81
  purified, 13
  wicked, 40, 57, 78
mind consciousness, 59
mind faculty, 59
mindfulness, 7, 19, 44, 65–66, 69–70, 72–74, 81, 84, 91
  confuse, 74
  cultivated, 81
  right, 12–13, 73
mindfulness-based cognitive therapy, 74
Mindfulness Based Relapse Prevention, 76
mindfulness practice, 71
mindfulness robbers, 74
misconduct, 12
  sexual, 2, 23, 37
miseries, 5, 27
mistress, 100
Modeled, 74
Mogallana, 89
moments, final, 51
monastic robes, 1
monastics, 22, 107
  helping, 107
money, 25, 49, 54, 65, 92, 95–97
  counterfeit, 96
  spending, 23
monks, 2–4, 7, 19, 21, 27, 40–41, 78, 87–88, 93–94, 107, 109
  arahant, 87, 89
  arrogant, 93
  senior, 87
monks and nuns, 107
monks chant, 88–89
Moral action, 37
moral conduct, 18
  good, 2
morality, 2, 4, 11, 14–15, 18, 37, 63–64
  observing, 66
  upholding, 1
moral life, 12, 64, 103
mortal kamma, 40–41
  powerful, 29
Moses, 100
mother, 40, 45, 104, 108–9
mother and father, 88, 101–3, 105
mother's bottle, 104
Motivation, 102
motive, 46–47, 96
motives, good, 96
mouth-diseases, 84
MRI, 45
MTA David, 60

Mundugumor tribe, 102
Muslim kamma, 29

N

nanoseconds, 51
Narcotics Anonymous, 69
natural interdependence, 14
natural law, 33–34, 47, 63–64, 94
natural phenomena, 44, 70
nature, 5, 7, 10, 15, 17–18, 43, 45–46, 54–55, 60, 65, 78, 84, 92
 real, 18
 true, 9–10, 14, 17, 37
 unitary, 60
nature ourselves, 18
necessities, basic, 95
nectar, 95
 flower-collecting, 95
negative consequences, 64
negative emotions, 74
negative power, 63
nervous system, 58
nervous vibrations, 53
neutral attitude, 10
Newborn babies and children, 102
New Jersey, 73
New Year's Day, 49
New York for surgery, 44
nibbana, 9, 11–12, 14–16, 37
 attained, 10
Noble Eightfold Path, 12, 14
noble truths, 12, 73
non-returner, 36
non-vegetarian, 94
non-vegetarian diet, 93
norms, 32, 91
 cultural, 103
 prescribed, 32
 social, 31
norms measure, 32
nose, 10, 59
nose-diseases, 84
nourish ourselves, 91
novice, young, 33
nuns, 21, 107, 109
nytimes.com, 69

O

obedience, 1, 66
objects, 2, 6, 10, 45, 54, 58–59, 83
 eye, 59
 mental, 59
 sense, 10
obligations, 9, 25, 33–34, 42, 55, 62, 95, 97
 matrimonial, 99
observances, 11, 19, 37
observation, 6
occasion, 30, 49, 83
once-returner, 36
Oregon, 44, 75
organ, powerful, 30
organizations, 69
origination, dependent, 71
outpatient clinics, 69
overpowering, 50

P

Pacific University, 75
pain, 30, 45–46, 72, 84
 bodily, 40
 extreme, 47
painkillers, 46–47
Pali, 73
Pali canon commentary, 35
Pali language, 60, 73
Pali word, 9
Pali word for mindfulness, 73
palpitations, 53
paññā, 1, 37
parent family, single, 105
parents, 24, 62, 66, 85, 88, 102–5
 single, 105
parents ourselves, 102

parks, public, 97
partner, 99, 106
PAT, 79
Patama sanvasa sutta, 106
path, 1–2, 6, 12–14, 23, 34, 51–52, 54, 62, 70, 77
    direct, 6, 13
patience, 37, 45
patient, 44, 46–47, 89–90, 96
    addicted, 71
patient recover, 46
paying bills, 25
paying government taxes, 25
paying taxes, 97
peace, 3–4, 34, 43, 47, 63, 77, 82, 90
peacefulness, 35
peace of mind, 11, 43
people's patterns, 77
perceptions, 42, 53, 59, 84
perfections, 37, 108–9
perfect wisdom, attained, 33
periods
    long, 29
    short, 33, 62
perpetuating, 78
persistent effort, 22–23
person, 9–10, 12, 14–15, 29–30, 35–38, 43, 47, 49–51, 53, 55, 58, 66–67, 69, 71–72, 78
    considerate, 45
    perfected, 78
    richest, 23
    skillful, 66
    worldly, 38
    young, 4, 28
personal decision, 100
personal experience, 7, 44
personal growth, 102
personality, 101–3
    children's, 102
person cultivates, 13
person damages, 70
person eats, 74
person intent, 39
person plucks, 97
person's mind, 41
    ordinary, 36
perspective
    particular, 60
    positive, 32
physical formation, 72
physical forms, 51
physical material, 6
physical phenomena, 72
physicians, 46, 79
    eye, 78
plants, 43, 92
plates, 91–92
police, 83, 104
police investigations, 83
pool, 6
Pope, 100
poverty, dreadful, 29
power, 1, 27–28, 31–32, 54, 72–73, 82, 88, 101
power cords, 28
practice
    daily, 90
    laywomen, 107
practice discipline, 15
practiced loving friendliness meditation, 45
practiced loving-friendliness meditation, 89
practice generosity, 2, 4, 11, 18, 25, 64
practice loving-kindness meditation, 94
practice mediation, 54
practice meditation, 2, 4
practice morality, 11
practice spirituality, 16
practitioners, 90
Prakrit, 73
pray, 4
precepts, 2, 4, 11, 18, 25, 36, 38–39, 42, 89
    five fundamental, 21

observing, 4, 30, 37
observing moral, 2
prevention, 106
mindfulness-based relapse, 74
Princess Hemamala, 108
prisons, 74, 83
private practice, 83
problems, 43–44, 77, 101
complex, 77
never-ending, 77
social, 101
process, 2, 5, 14–16, 27, 72, 100
complete existence, 71
long, 9, 13
long growth, 16
natural, 5
processes unfolding, 75
professions, 94, 103
prognosis, 44–45
doctor's, 44
promise, 74, 83
prospective partners, 106
protection, 102–3
Protestant dominations, 100
psychological incompatibility, 101
punna, 38
puñña, 35
pupils, 41
pure mind, 13, 42, 57–58, 67, 96
pure thought, 13
pure words, 11
Purification, 51–52
purify, 11, 18, 35, 89
purity, 13, 54
pyramid, five-level, 102

Q

qualification, 9
qualities, 1–4, 13–14, 22–23, 31, 66, 77, 81
good, 3
positive, 66
quoted response, 99

R

rainy season, 78
realization, 7, 14
rebirth, 28, 41, 51
recitations, common, 90
reciting, 90
reciting suttas, 87
Recollecting, 38
recollection, 73
recover, 46, 76, 82, 84
recovery, 69–70, 103–4
patient's, 47
permanent, 69
wife's, 50
recovery programs, 69, 104
recovery rates, lowest, 74
reduction, 65, 71, 75
mindfulness-based stress, 74
Refuges, 90
region, 17, 32
regret, 38, 40
reject, 10, 32, 59
reject sense objects, 10
relapse, 74–76
lower risk of, 75–76
relationships, healthy, 103
relatives, 24, 60, 89, 97
best, 83
reliance, strong, 14
religion, 1, 4–5, 17, 19, 32, 100
particular, 33
religious activities, 97
religious legal systems, 32
renewal cycles, 51
Reno, 101
renunciation, 37
repercussions, 63
reproducing, 91
reputation, 102
good, 7
residency requirement, 101
responsibilities, 62, 102, 107, 109

restaurants, 92
Reverend Sir, 3
reverse order, 72
right action, 12
right concentration, 12–13
right effort, 12
right livelihood, 12, 23
rituals, 1, 31
road rage, 41
robberies, 85, 104
Roman Catholic Church, 100
roots, 35, 64, 74
  unwholesome, 35
RTA, 83, 85
RY, 71, 73, 75

S

safety, 41, 102
sale, 45
salutations, 90
samsaric journey, 37, 108
  person's, 30
sanctuaries, 97
sangha, 7, 90
Sanghamitta Theri, 108
Sanskrit, 73
Sanskrit smrti, 73
sati, 73
savior, 15, 18
school, 41, 60, 87, 104
  elementary, 9
  high, 9, 60
  middle, 9
science-based practices, 69
Scotland, 101
Scottish divorce, 101
security, 61, 90, 102–3
self, 73
  permanent, 84
self-actualization, 102
self-centeredness, 93
self-centered perspective, 14
self-collectedness, 73
self-control, 4
self-enlightenment, perfect, 3
self-esteem, 70
self-indulgence, 21
self-mortification, 21
self-mortification period, 81
self-restraint, 7
sensations, 42, 53, 58, 72
  pleasant bodily, 81
  pleasurable, 70
  single, 2
sense organs, 59
sermon, good, 109
servants, 3, 79, 97
service industries, 96
service occupations, 97
services, 62, 96–97
  commemorative, 55
  social, 97
seventeenth centuries, 100
sex, 102
  unlawful, 32–33
shadow, 23, 57
shafts, 33
  fletchers use, 33
Shameless exposure of body, 70
shelter, 25, 95, 97, 102
shopping, 92, 94
short-circuit, 75
sicknesses, 46, 52, 84, 87, 92
  mental, 81–82
  painful, 91
  physical, 61, 81–82, 84
Siddhartha, 82
Siddhartha Gautama, 15
Sigala, 70, 103
sight, 21, 59, 78–79
Sigmund Freud, 101
sīla, 1, 37
Singhalovada Discourse, 24
situations
  sorrowful, 40

special, 31
unhappy, 30
sixteenth century, early, 100
skills, 33, 57, 67
basic, 62
complex, 31
social, 62
wholesome, 35
skin-disease, 84
sleep, 25, 31, 90, 102
smell, 10, 21, 51, 59, 81
social beings, 24
social circle, 37
social milieu, 60
society, 2, 28, 32, 43, 58, 61–63, 65, 82, 101, 103, 105
civil, 104
civilized, 44
modern, 92, 104
particular, 32
stable, 32
son, 1, 22–23, 88, 100
out-of-wedlock, 100
sounds, 10, 21, 59, 90
sound waves, 89
specializations, 31
speech, 3, 27
harmful, 65
right, 11–12
slanderous, 12
speeding, 41
spiritual activities, 45
spiritual choices, 70
spiritual environment, 11
deep, 11
spiritualties, 15
sporting activities, 42
Sri Dhammananda, 57–58
Sri Lanka, 108
planted, 108
stability, 102–3
start, maggots, 54
start earning, 62
started drinking alcohol, 104
started selling drugs, 104
started work, 60
state, 9, 12–14, 16, 22, 36–37, 45, 57–58, 99–101
distinct momentary, 58
evil, 77
mundane, 36
nation, 32
unwholesome, 13
verse, 57
state welfare assistance, 104
stomach, 92–93
stomach-ache, 84
story, 4, 23–24, 33, 40, 45, 78, 82–83, 89, 97
short, 78
stream-enterer, 36
strength, 29, 91
relative, 29
strenuous effort, 14
stress, 2, 4, 16, 25, 35, 61–65, 67, 101
increased, 66
managing, 61, 66
negative, 64
reducing, 62
unexplained, 64
stress and anxiety, 4, 61, 65, 67
stress level, 105
stress management, 61, 63
stress-related illnesses, 62
stress relievers, 63
strides, rapid, 77
subject, 5–6, 51–52, 59
substance abuse recovery, 73
substance use, 74–76
days of, 75–76
succession, rapid, 51
suicide, 43–44, 46–47, 50, 63, 101
committing, 39
human, 43
physician-assisted, 44
suicide assistance, 46
sun, 15, 103

sunshine, 15, 22
superhuman, 14
supernatural power, 1
superpower, 4, 7, 30
support, 21, 29, 44–45, 95, 104
surgeon, 46, 96
surgery, 44–47
surroundings, 89
survival, 91, 94
Susceptibility, 70
suttas, 87
swallowing, 74
switches, 27–28
sympathetic joy, 14, 67, 78–79, 96, 102

T

taboos, 32, 49, 91, 103
tame, 15, 57
tank, 25
taste, 10, 21, 51, 59
taste appetizing foods, 81
teachers, 7, 15, 17–18, 33, 60, 83, 85, 96, 103, 109
teacher's request, 40
teachings, 6–7, 13, 18, 58, 73, 87, 106, 108–9
  edit Buddha's, 7
  good, 4
techniques, 39, 61, 63–65, 70
  good, 64
  good management, 64
  reducing recreational, 63
technological aids, 61
technology, 77
teenagers, 62, 69
teeth-diseases, 84
temples, 19, 97, 108
Thich Nguyen Tang, 54
Thich Nhat Hanh, 73
thirst, 22, 72, 84
thoughtless, 5
Thou shall not commit adultery, 100
time laboring, long, 95
time management, 65–66
time meditating, 45
tissues liquefy, 54
tolerance, 45, 79
  high, 38
tongue, 10, 59
tongue-diseases, 84
tools, 31, 76
Tooth, 108
tooth relic, 108
Tooth Relic Temple, 108
topic, 49, 69
total blindness, permanent, 79
tradition, unbroken, 87
traditional, 74, 76
Traditional chanting, 90
traffic accidents, 41, 63
transcendent, 1
transformative wisdom, 3
translations, 28
transportation, 96
Treating Addiction, 74
treatment, 69–70, 74, 83
  cognitive behavioral, 69
  effective addiction, 69
  equal, 4
  spiritual, 69
treatment centers, 74
treatment protocol targets, 74
Tree, Bodhi, 108
trivial pursuits, 65
truth, 1, 7, 12, 15, 17, 67, 87–89
  absolute, 67
  ultimate, 17
truthfulness, 37
tuberculosis, 84
Twist, 41

U

unattractiveness, 84
uncomfortable procedures, 46